Twayne's United States Authors Series

Sylvia E. Bowman, *Editor*

INDIANA UNIVERSITY

Paddy Chayefsky

TUSAS 272

Paddy Chayefsky

PADDY CHAYEFSKY

By JOHN M. CLUM

Duke University

TWAYNE PUBLISHERS
A DIVISION OF G. K. HALL & CO., BOSTON

Library of Congress Cataloging in Publication Data

Clum, John M
  Paddy Chayefsky.

  (Twayne's United States authors series; TUSAS
272)
  Bibliography: p. 143–45.
  Includes index.
  1. Chayefsky, Paddy, 1923-
PS3505.H632Z56   812'.5'4   76-7363
ISBN 0-8057-7172-7

In Memoriam
ALAN SEYMOUR DOWNER

Contents

About the Author

John M. Clum, an Associate Professor of English at Duke University and Director of the Duke University Drama Program, received his A.B. and Ph.D. from Princeton University. His fields of interest are American drama and film. Professor Clum is the author of the Twayne's United States Authors Series volume on Ridgely Torrence as well as articles on American drama and higher education. He received Duke's Outstanding Professor Award in 1969 and has over the past ten years at Duke taught over twenty different courses and directed over a score of dramatic productions, two of which he co-authored.

Preface

Paddy Chayefsky is one of that rare breed of contemporary play-wrights who has been able to combine considerable commercial success with artistic respectability. Moreover, his situation is unique in that his success has come in three media. He became famous through his plays for television; for, during that tragically short period in which television was the purveyor of exciting original drama, Chayefsky was rightfully considered the medium's finest writer. His success in television led to film offers; and his *Marty*, an adaptation of a television script, became one of the most highly acclaimed films of the 1950's. The mastery of the film medium demonstrated by the screenplay for *Marty* led to many successful scripts including those for such films as *The Goddess* and *Hospital*. In fact, Chayefsky is a rarity — a screenwriter who receives star billing. The next world to conquer was the stage, and Chayefsky began again with an adaptation of a television success, *Middle of the Night*. This success was followed by a variety of plays quite different from his television work.

Chayefsky's versatility is not only demonstrated by his success in various media but proven by his ability to write effectively within a number of varying styles. The television plays were beautiful, small-scale examples of the middle-class Realistic drama developed by Clifford Odets and Arthur Miller. These dramas about the claustrophobia felt by sensitive individuals trapped within humdrum lives were perfectly suited to the small, grey screen. They were nicely etched character sketches brought to life by a fine ear for the nuances and rhythms of everyday urban speech and by a good sense of the relationships that characterized second-generation families packed together in urban tenements.

The early films and plays retained the virtues of their video counterparts, but they were successful in their own right because

Chayefsky's sense of color and balance allowed him to "open out" his plays to great advantage. For example, *Marty* and *Middle of the Night* were converted from successful charcoal sketches to finely detailed paintings in which the environment became a crucial character, and secondary characters allowed the audience to see the frustrations of the principals in their proper social perspective. Chayefsky was not content to repeat himself, however successfully; and his later plays and films are much larger in scale and more spiritual in content. Where *Marty* and *Middle of the Night* depict simple people grappling with mundane issues of everyday life — homeliness, loneliness, age — *The Tenth Man* and *Gideon* dramatize deeper spiritual issues — spiritual emptiness and man's relationship to God. In Chayefsky's later, more successful works, *The Latent Heterosexual* and *The Hospital*, the author deals on a large scale with what he now sees as the basic question of his age — how one can survive relatively intact in a mad world in which one's individuality is constantly threatened.

Chayefsky's career is noteworthy, then, not only for its variety and richness but also for its demonstration of the mastery of the writer's craft. Chayefsky's characters merge the particular and the universal: a lonely Bronx butcher who comes to represent the beauty that underlies the less than glamorous exteriors of most people; a middle-aged businessman who embodies the fear of losing his manhood with his youth; or a successful doctor to whom the entire world seems terminally ill. Moreover, these characters are given dialogue that seems at one with their personalities, whether their speech is the accurate realization of a Bronx dialect or the breathless, witty flights of rhetoric that characterize Chayefsky's more recent heroes.

Above all, Chayefsky is an experimenter; he never settles for the same formula twice, and he is willing to take incredible chances in the structuring of his work. Like many contemporary writers, he is willing to mix styles and genres within the same work; and, with Chayefsky, the effect is usually that of a unified conception. His vision of the world has grown darker over the years, but it is always balanced by a brilliant, caustic sense of humor.

This is the first full-length study of Chayefsky's work to date. Despite the fact that it covers one-hour television dramas, screenplays, and full-scale dramatic conceptions, one can see consistent lines of development as Chayefsky progresses from a "slice of life" Realist to a dark satirist who has absorbed the best of the developments in contemporary theater. Always, one sees the product of a meticulous craftsman.

Chayefsky's output is not large, yet it poses problems of organization. Since my first concern was to be as complete as possible, every television play written for the "Philco Television Playhouse" is discussed except "Middle of the Night" which is discussed in detail as a stage play. Every produced stage work is discussed, as well as a fine, early, unproduced work, "Fifth from Garibaldi"; and every screenplay — except the disastrous adaptation of *Paint Your Wagon* — is extensively examined. A problem arose in dealing with works that appear in two or three media; but, having decided to organize Chayefsky's works by genre rather than strict chronological order, I then established the policy of dealing extensively with a work in its published version. Other versions of the same work are discussed only in terms of additions or changes made in translating them from one medium to another.

Since there is no published edition of Chayefsky's screenplays (with the exception of *The Goddess*), I was dependent upon the generosity of Mr. Chayefsky and the staff of the State Historical Society of Wisconsin for many of my texts. Thank heaven for the Xerox machine!

By the time this volume appears, there will be yet another Chayefsky film in release (the shooting script is discussed in Chapter 4). His canon is far from complete. This book, then, marks the first twenty-five years of a remarkable career.

JOHN M. CLUM

Duke University

Acknowledgments

I am deeply grateful to Paddy Chayefsky for his generous co-operation in providing advice and material for this study. Thanks, too, to Eleanor McKay of the Wisconsin State Historical Society for her invaluable assistance. Indeed, the entire staff of the Manuscript / Archives Division of the Society is a model for this type of organization.

Thanks, too, to Richard Kuhn for his assistance in gathering data and to Virginia Bossons for her generous assistance in preparing the manuscript. Richard Cytowic was, as usual, a great help in the editorial "dirty work."

Chronology

1923   Sidney Chayefsky born January 29 in New York City.

1939   January, graduates from DeWitt Clinton High School, Bronx. Enters City College of New York.

1940   Plays semi-professional football for the Knightsbridge Trojans.

1943   Graduates from City College of New York. Joins 104th Infantry Division.

1944   Wounded by a land mine in Germany. Writes musical, "No T.O. for Love" while recuperating in English hospital. Receives Purple Heart.

1945   "No T.O. for Love" produced for Special Services tour with Chayefsky in leading role. Works on film, *The True Glory*.

1946   Discharged from army. Works in uncle's print shop. Awarded $500 writing fellowship by Garson Kanin. Studies at the Actor's Lab in Hollywood. Writes play, "Put Them All Together."

1947   Awarded Junior Writer's contract with Universal-International.

1949   Story, "The Great American Hoax," published by *Cosmopolitan*.

1950   Writes play, "The Man Who Made the Mountains Shake."

1952   Begins writing radio plays for "Theater Guild of the Air" and "Cavalcade of America." Writes television scripts for *Danger* and *Manhunt*. "Philco Television Playhouse" productions of "Holiday Song" and "The Reluctant Citizen."

1953   "Philco Television Playhouse" produces "Printer's Measure," "Marty," "The Big Deal," "The Bachelor Party," "The Sixth Year," "Catch My Boy on Sunday."

1954   "The Mother" and "Middle of the Night" presented on "Philco Television Playhouse." Film version of *Marty* released.

1955   *Marty* wins four Academy Awards including Best Screenplay and Best Picture. "A Catered Affair" is his last play for television.

1956   *Middle of the Night* opens on Broadway with Edward G. Robinson.

1957   Film version of *The Bachelor Party* released.

1958   *The Goddess* released; wins critics' prize at Brussels Film Festival.

1959   Film version of *Middle of the Night* released in New York and London. *The Tenth Man* becomes second Broadway success. Chayefsky travels to Russia to speak with Russian writers under auspices of the United States' State Department.

1961   *Gideon* opens in New York.

1964   *The Passion of Josef D.*, written and directed by Chayefsky, opens. *The Americanization of Emily*, with screenplay by Chayefsky, is released in New York.

1968   *The Latent Heterosexual* is produced in Dallas, Los Angeles, and at the Bristol Old Vic in England.

1970   Writes screenplay for film adaptation of *Paint Your Wagon*.

1971   Television version of *Gideon*. *The Hospital* released. Chayefsky helps found Writers and Artists for Peace in the Middle East. Delegate to International Conference on Soviet Jewry.

1972   *The Hospital* wins Academy Award for Best Screenplay.

1976   *Network* filmed in New York.

CHAPTER 1

Learning the Trade

M Y writing of *Paddy Chayefsky* began, coincidentally, on his
fiftieth birthday — an age that is young for a man but not for
a major American playwright. Our playwrights tend to be lionized
for their early work and then mourned for their later failure to equal
their first successes. Chayefsky, now fifty-three, is at the height of
his career. His screenplay, *The Hospital* won him the Academy
Award in 1972, as did his first, *Marty*, two decades ago in 1955. He
has been celebrated for his work in three media, and he is constantly
breaking new ground in his handling of both style and content. And,
like many well-known American authors, Chayefsky has become a
personality in his own right. His driving ambition, his pride in his
work, and his persistence in protecting his conceptions have made
him a controversial figure in the performing arts. More important is
the fact that his work has developed as has his own progressively
darkening vision of life's possibilities.

I   *The Early Years*

Next to the picture of Class Wit Sidney Q. Chayefsky (the "Q" a
fictional embellishment) in the January, 1939, DeWitt Clinton High
School Yearbook, there is a forthright but unique design for the
young man's future, "Muckraking." This ambition may have been as
fictional as the middle initial Chayefsky gave himself, but it catches
our eye as we pore over those noble aspirations that fill high school
yearbooks.

The future muckraker was the youngest son of Russian-born parents who had emigrated to the United States in their teens and who
had met at Coney Island, of all places. Although Harry and Gussie
Chayefsky were not formally educated people, they had a Central

European love for the arts and a respect for education. Harry played the mandolin and relished taking his three sons to the Yiddish Theater where young Sidney no doubt saw S. Ansky's classic, *The Dybbuk*, which later became the basis for *The Tenth Man*. Gussie insisted on piano lessons and good grades for all her children. Young Sidney was a good student with, he later claimed, "the highest I.Q. in the city."[1]

When Sidney was born on January 29, 1923, the Chayefskys were living in some affluence. Harry, who had begun his American career as a milkman, was now an executive with Dellwood Dairies. The Depression hit his business, however, and he was never so successful again as he was during Sidney's boyhood. In 1930, the father sold his dairy to avoid bankruptcy and tried the building business, but without success. Finally, Harry got a steady job as manager of a creamery; but, despite the changing fortunes of the family, most of Sidney's youth was spent in the middle-class Riverdale section of the Bronx. What he saw, heard, and experienced there during his youth served him well later as the basis for his early literary successes.

Chayefsky's neighborhood, like most of those in the Bronx, was peopled by immigrants and their children: "I came from a mixed neighborhood. There were Jewish families and Italian and Irish families. There is a distinct similarity between their homes — very close family ties among emotionally volatile people."[2] He studied Hebrew and worshiped in a modest synagogue much like the one in his *The Tenth Man*. He was a shy, quiet, young man, though the title of Class Wit suggests that his sense of humor already was flourishing. He was editor of his high school literary magazine, *The Magpie*; but Seymour Krim, his predecessor as editor, says that Sidney's contributions to the magazine seemed rather crass to his esthetically oriented peers who disdained Chayefsky's down-to-earth contributions and his ambition to be a commercial writer. Krim told one interviewer, "We were pretty condescending, but our criticisms rolled right off his back. He wasn't the least bit swayed by us, and I must say he was far more realistic. He was making money writing burlesque skits."[3]

Sidney Q. attended the City College of New York after graduating from DeWitt Clinton High School, and his avid interest in literature was fed by reading the playwrights then called "modern" — Henrik Ibsen, Anton Chekhov, and G. B. Shaw — and by studying with

Professor Teddy Goodman in his renowned playwrighting course, English 12, which was City College's counterpart to George Pierce Baker's 47 Workshop at Harvard. For a short time, his academic career was augmented by his performance for the Knightsbridge Trojans, a semi-professional football team; but he soon found that the risks were too great for a five foot six football player. After Chayefsky was graduated from college in 1943, he, like most of his peers, found himself in the war; but, for the budding writer, World War II led to some great opportunities. After sending him to Fordham to learn German, the army assigned Chayefsky to the 104th Infantry Division where his army career was cut short by a land mine. During his stay in the army, Chayefsky was dubbed "Paddy" by an officer who was amused at the Jewish soldier's attempts to get out of kitchen duty to attend Catholic mass. One army friend remarked, "Until I met Chayefsky, I thought I was the sloppiest soldier in the Army. Bedraggled is the best description — his shirttail always riding out of his pants and one trouser leg always out of the boot."[4]

After the land mine accident at Aachen, Chayefsky was shipped to a London hospital where he and a fellow patient, composer Jimmy Livingston, began writing a musical called "No T.O. [Table of Organization] for Love." The script crossed the desk of actor Curt Conway, who was then assigned to produce Special Services shows for soldiers in London. Conway found the script ". . . very dirty, full of latrine humor. But still, it was one of the most clearly talented things I'd read in a long time."[5] The show was produced in London and Paris with Chayefsky in a leading role (he told me that he had to act in the show to avoid being sent back to the front), and it was a great success. Author-director Garson Kanin was among many theater people who saw "No T.O. for Love," and he was happy to have Chayefsky assigned to work with him on a documentary about the war entitled *The True Glory*. The film was an international venture that also involved the talents of Peter Ustinov and Claude Dauphin.

After the war, Chayefsky returned to the states; earned some money by working in his uncle's print shop (the basis for his teleplay, "Printers' Measure"); and was the recipient of a five hundred dollar fellowship from Garson Kanin who had great faith in the promising writer's talent. The next six years were times of trial and error for the young man who was eager to make his mark in some area of show business. Under the auspices of Kanin's fellowship, he wrote a full-length play, "Put Them All Together," which Kanin optioned. The play tells of a larger-than-life woman's efforts to hold on to her two sons, one of whom is an aspiring writer. The setting is the Bronx, and the play is an attempt to capture the flavor of locale and speech that would eventually be Chayefsky's trademark. We find in this script Chayefsky's remarkable ear for dialogue and his ability to depict domestic crises.

Although "Put Them All Together" was never produced, it did attract the attention of a number of producers including Mike Gordon and Jerry Bressler who offered Chayefsky a Junior Writer's contract in Hollywood. Chayefsky already had some film experience not only with *The True Glory*, but also through his studies at the Actor's Lab in Hollywood under the G.I. Bill of Rights and in his small role in a Ronald Coleman epic, *Double Life*, written by Garson Kanin and his wife, Ruth Gordon. Under Chayefsky's new contract, he wrote the scenario "The Great American Hoax" which was about a man's masquerading as president of General Motors. While he sold the story to *Cosmopolitan* in 1949, his scenario was never produced, though, much to the author's dismay, it became the basis of a later film with Monty Wooley, *As Young as You Feel*, and a teleplay with Ed Wynn.

Discouraged by lack of progress in Hollywood, Chayefsky returned to New York and supported himself with a number of odd jobs. He was, for a very brief time, a gag writer for comedian Robert Q. Lewis, who remarked that "Chayefsky was the first writer I ever had who looked like he was here on a football scholarship."[6] Whatever Chayefsky's appearance, his job with Lewis was short-lived: "I got fired — on very friendly terms. I just couldn't write gags."[7] Lewis may not have been happy with Chayefsky's gags, but they did provide their author with his own material for dates as a stand-up comic. These odd jobs helped support him while he labored on another play, "The Man Who Made the Mountains Shake" (later titled "Fifth from Garibaldi"), which caught the attention of Elia Kazan whose wife, Molly, helped Chayefsky with the revisions. Again, when sufficient money could not be raised to produce the play, Chayefsky was frustrated and somewhat embittered by his inability to get his work before the public and to gain the recognition he so desired. Unsuccessful with drama, he tried prose fiction; but his work in this area, including a novella "Go Fight City Hall," was returned with rejection slips.

Although to delve deeply into the unpublished apprentice work of a writer produces little more than scholarly esoterica, and although the focus of this study is upon the produced and published work of Paddy Chayefsky, we can understand Chayefsky's artistic origins best by looking at a few of his early pieces — particularly at the play "Fifth from Garibaldi" — and at some of his prose works.

II *The Legacy of Odets*

A number of critics over the years have compared Chayefsky's work to Clifford Odets' best work. Odets was interested in creating realistic dramas that would expose the weaknesses of the capitalist system. Whatever we think of his philosophy, he managed in his best work — plays like *Paradise Lost*, *Awake and Sing*, and *Golden Boy* — to capture the language and the futility of the urban poor, the people who are so crucial to Chayefsky's work during the 1950's. Nowhere is the relationship between the two writers more striking than it is in Chayefsky's play, "Fifth from Garibaldi," which is the final revision of a play originally titled "The Man Who Made the Mountains Shake." The final version was completed in 1952; and, though it never reached production, it shows many of the best qualities of Chayefsky's Realistic work.

The play takes place in an Italian-American neighborhood of Boston, a city in which non–Anglo-Saxons were not absorbed so effectively as they were in cities like New York. The time is 1922; and the Fortunatos, the family the play depicts, are typical in maintaining an uneasy balance between the Old World and the New. As Chayefsky tells us in the Preface, "The people who live in the Italian colony of Boston are simple people who feel uncomfortable beyond the confines of their dense little community and cling to their old cultural identity with a sense of desperation."[8]

In his environment, Mario Fortunato, the fifty-year-old head of the household, is a proud man who rules his humble house like an old country don. He prides himself upon his strength, a strength which once made mountains shake:

There was a stone inna field outside the village of Avalino, where I was born. The stone was the size of a man. Nobody could pick up this stone. . . . Finally, somebody says, hey, anybody gonna pick up this stone, that's

Mario Fortunato. I was big, and I was handsome. I had muscles in my back you could see for a hundred yards. . . . Sunday afternoon I went out inna field. The whole village was there. Alla women on the side waiting to see if I'm gonna pick up this stone. So I put my arm around it. Ohhhh . . . I pick it up! I felt in that moment in my heart something mysterious. And just then, the mountain shook! Mount Vesuvius, the volcano, she began to shake! God! You gave me the strength of angels. (I-35)

But the "strength of angels" is wasted in a humiliating job as a ditchdigger in the Navy Yard, and Mario's pride and dignity, which seem to be ebbing away, are being replaced by a sense of helplessness: "I tell you! . . . I feel I am in somebody's hand, and they squeezing my bones! (2-18).

Mario's hope is in his sons — that at least one of them will use his inherited strength to become a boxing champion. Right now, his hopes of glory ride with his son Vinnie who already has seventeen "knock-outs" on his record: "You tell my father that my son Vinnie has my great strength, and, before he dies, my father will hear Mussolini say his name inna speech" (2-22). But Vinnie, sick from a concussion received in a fight the night before, decides he wants a safer, more reliable job as a truck driver: "I don't like to fight! I don't like to go inna stinking dressing room! I don't like to get inna ring! I don't like the noise! I don't like the smella the rosin! . . . Whaddaya want from me, Pa? I don't wanna fight . . . that's all . . . I wanna getta job. . ." (2-31).

Vinnie's defiance of Mario's fondest dream leaves the father in despair. Mario needs the dreams of his son's championship to maintain his pride, just as he needs to feel, according to his wife, that he made the mountains shake: "Don't you think that he believes he made the mountains shake? Don't you think he believes that? My God! That's his whole life, that mountain! He would be a ghost without that mountain! That man is fifty-one years old. He's a ditchdigger inna Navy Yard. He has to believe something, don't he?" (2-39). His wife, Lucy, understands her husband, just as she understands why her boys should box: "You think I want my son to be a fighter? But you gotta be practical. I mean, what can an Italian boy do in this city? Work inna Navy Yard and groan all his life?" (1-4). When Mario's dreams are shattered and he is full of self-pity and of hatred for the sons who disappointed him, Lucy tells him he will only be happy when he settles for what he has: "Mario, you have seven sons who adore you. Can Mussolini boast of more glory than that?" (B-6). Mario must stop building his self-image on his legendary strength: "My God, Mario, do you really believe God made the mountain shake for you? . . . My God, Mario, Vesuvius shakes ten times a year without you. . . . Now you just gotta siddown and say to yourself, Mario Fortunato, I am a guinea ditchdigger, poor wop, and I tell you on my soul, Mario, you gonna be a happy man . . ." (3-8).

Mario is not ready to accept Lucy's advice until he sees his son Tony, a frail, sickly adolescent, try to shoot himself because he lost his first fight through weakness and terror: "Will you destroy yourself for this foolish vanity! Whatsa matter with you. This is my sin. . . . Boy, we say in Italian — if a horse tells you he is Queen of Spain, you put a saddle on his back anyway. . . . I'm a fool, boy, but that don't mean you gotta believe me" (3-13). Mario Fortunato finally recognizes that he is the fortunate one, for he is loved. Next to the love of his son, the glory he cherishes is mere fantasy.

In "Fifth from Garibaldi," Chayefsky has created a touching story of a man who is lost in the New World. Mario Fortunato had come to America to become wealthy and important; but, like many of his friends, he is no better off than he was in the old country. His solace is his strength and his dreams of his sons' success. Chayefsky's interest is not in the economic poverty of his characters but in its relative unimportance, for the point of "Fifth from Garibaldi" is that Mario's, or any person's, estimate of his worth and the love he gives to and receives from those around him are the things that count. This solution is quite a contrast to Clifford Odets' solution in *Golden Boy*, a play which bears many surface resemblances to Chayefsky's play. The Bonaparte family of Odets' play is also a poor urban Italian family; and Mr. Bonaparte, a fruit vendor, has great dreams for his son, Joe. He has just spent all his savings on a violin for Joe, but his son does not want to make music anymore. There is no money in art, but there is plenty in fighting, so Joe becomes a boxer: "Do you know there are men who have wonderful things from life? Do you think they're better than me? Do you think I like this feeling of no possessions?"[9]

Joe Bonaparte becomes a champion; but, as a result, he loses all the characteristics that make him human: he has been sold as a commodity, and he himself loves only his fast car. By the time he realizes the extent to which he has sacrificed his humanity, it is too late; and he dies, wrecked in his beloved car, while trying to escape the trap his life has become. Odets' family in *Golden Boy* is one for whom money is everything. The father's savings have bought the violin, son-in-law Siggie is constantly looking for ways to "get ahead," and son Frank is a labor agitator fighting for better wages and hours for his comrades. The ideal is not to exult in the non-material things since that is impossible, but to find or make a new world that is not ruled by materialism: "Somewhere there must be happy boys and girls who can teach us the way of life! We'll find some city where poverty's no shame — where music is no crime — where there's no war in the streets — where a man is glad to be himself, to live and make his woman herself."[10] Frank sees correctly that this brighter world must be forged out of the present one.

Odets is not so much interested in his characters as people as he is in their polemic value, for we are given no noneconomic reason for a sensitive, cross-eyed young man's conversion from the violin to the boxing ring. Though Joe talks of his need to be free of his father, we see only a kind, concerned old man. To the young people in the play, happiness is bought with money; and we sense that Odets believes that, if only everyone had enough money, all would be well. No one would be ambitious or greedy, and people could then be free.

Both Chayefsky and Odets offer, therefore, somewhat one-sided solutions to the problems of the New World. Mario Fortunato's realization of the value of love does not make his job any less humiliating, and he still has many mouths to feed. Neither, how-ever, does Odets' murky Utopian Socialism explain Joe Bonaparte's ambition or his misfortunes. What both men do capture is the lan-guage of the people they depict as well as the vitality of the types they dramatize, but Chayefsky's early work triumphs over its better known predecessor in its warmth. Odets is always somewhat clinical about his characters — their mendacity eliminates any sympathetic qualities they may have, and their statements become overly didac-tic. The Fortunato family lives from the heart, and its story is a celebration of human feeling — of a family's love for its father and of a man's despair that turns to joy. This family play makes no pretense to solve the world's problems, but it makes us feel with the For-tunatos. No allegory exists, for boxing is not, as it is in *Golden Boy*, the cosmic battle to get ahead — it is a man's using his strength to gain glory and eight dollars minus carfare. To Chayefsky, the lives of the characters count, not their social implications.

Both Chayefsky and Odets are champions of the "little man" in their Realistic works; however, Chayefsky celebrates what such a man is, while Odets hopes for his improvement through social change. By the time Chayefsky began writing, the Socialist Realism of the Group Theater was replaced by the intense psychological Realism of the Actors' Studio; and, since studio-adherent Elia Kazan was most interested in Chayefsky's play, this new emphasis was most influential on Chayefsky's work in the 1950's. Although a number of years were to pass before a Chayefsky play was produced in New York, "Fifth from Garibaldi" proved his promise as a playwright and established his place in the tradition of American Realism.

III   *Prose Pieces*

Chayefsky, who has only published two pieces of fiction during his career, wrote both stories before he received recognition as a playwright; and they were published ten years apart: "The Great American Hoax," in *Cosmopolitan* in 1949; "The Giant Fan," in *Harper's Bazaar* a decade later. The histories of these stories are quite interesting, and the stories show two contrasting sides of Chayefsky's writing — sentimental humor and Naturalism — that were to merge to create his most successful work. "The Great American Hoax" is a shorter version of a novella entitled "A Few Kind Words from Newark," which Chayefsky wrote as a rendering for a screenplay. Ultimately, the story was adapted for the screen by someone else and not to Chayefsky's satisfaction.

"A Few Kind Words from Newark" tells the story of a sixty-five-year-old handpress operator who loses his job because of an edict from the owner of his plant that men must retire at sixty-five. In the process of protesting this edict which robs him of his beloved work and his livelihood, John Hodges discovers that the Acme Printing Service for which he works is "a subsidiary of the Cincinnati Publishing Service, whose stock was held by the Stimson Iron Foundry, Inc., which in turn had been recently swallowed up in the merger by the Bullock-Finch Nut and Bolt Co., Inc., whose parent organization was American Hardware, Inc., Ltd., whose directorate was interlocked with that of Allied Steel, Inc., which was one of the subsidiaries of the incredibly complex corporate structure, General Motors."[11] Hodges also discovers that no one seems to know who runs General Motors: "This is a complicated society in which a man would recognize Cary Grant on a subway, but he doesn't even know the name of his boss" (22).

The loss of his job and the discovery of the anonymity of the men who control his business give Hodges a scheme to save his job. He will print some General Motors stationery and send a letter on it stating that Charles Wilson, President of General Motors, is paying a visit to the Acme Printing Service. He does so; and, on the appointed date, John Hodges appears in Newark as Charles Wilson, tells the management of the Acme Printing Service to re-instate the men who had been forcibly retired, and regains his own job. Hodges-Wilson is also asked to speak before the Newark Chamber of Commerce, and his heart-felt plea for the dignity of age is given nationwide coverage that alerts the real Charles Wilson, All, of course, ends happily.

"A Few Kind Words from Newark" is a delightful work, not so much for its simple plot as for the delightful secondary characters — the over-romantic boss's wife, the harassed son, and the neurotic clerk with five shares of General Motors and delusions of grandeur. The story abounds in sub-plots that involve these delightful types and emerges as one of those instances in which the whole is better than the sum of its many and varied parts. The best moments are those of dialogue, for Chayefsky is not a very effective descriptive writer. He seldom gives a strong sense of place, and seldom in his fiction is he careful about chronology.

The basic theme of the novella is one that Chayefsky would use over and over — that of the man who will stage a seemingly quixotic battle to maintain his position in an impersonal world. As Hodges' granddaughter tells him, "All of a sudden it came to me, like a burst of lightning, that nothing is more important than your dignity. It's more important than a high standard of living or being assistant to the head. And that's what this was all about wasn't it? You were fighting for your dignity, the dignity of your work. You were going to fight the whole complex world for your dignity" (75). This same struggle motivates the principal characters in many of Chayefsky's later works — from "Printer's Measure" to *Marty* to *Gideon* and even *The Hospital*.

Chayefsky's second story, "The Giant Fan," paints a far less rosy picture of the world than the earlier story. No other work of Chayefsky's is quite as bleak and hopeless as this short tale of the colorless life of Edgar Castle whose story begins and ends with acts of violence. In a frighteningly matter-of-fact, reportorial style, Chayefsky gives us the first twenty-nine years of a young man from the Bronx who seems unable to live a life that is in any way meaningful. Edgar "grew older under the illusion he was going to be something,"[12] but he had no idea of how to master circumstances— except in his fantasy life. Edgar dreams of being a doctor, but biology makes him sick; he sees himself as a lawyer, but without a college degree. Forced by his family's financial position to go to work after college, Edgar felt trapped in a mundane routine: "He had a constant desire to bolt from wherever he was and hitchhike to another part of the country" (182). His four years in the army during World War II only taught him to accept his position as an anonymous, will-less cog in a machine; and he returned home only to find himself once again trapped in the banality of his job as a taxi driver; his small, hot tenement; his loveless marriage; and his liquor and fantasies of success mingled with self-pity: "I'm no good. I'm no good. What am I? I'm a goddamn hackie, a bum. I'm no good" (183).

Edgar's childhood was devoted to baseball; but his fervor for his favorite team, the New York Giants, transcended a boy's normal enthusiasm. At the age of twelve, he beat a Dodger fan over the head with a brief case full of books. After a hiatus of some years, twenty-nine-year-old Edgar Castle rediscovers the New York Giants; and he has pride and a feeling of identification with the men who are "somebody." The New York Giants gave Edgar an identity, albeit an ephemeral one. He could share in their triumphs and thus forget his own lack of success. They also, unfortunately, gave him something to fight for. On August 11, Edgar Castle beat a customer over the head with a coin changer because the man claimed that Robinson was a better second baseman than Stanky.

"The Giant Fan" is indeed a grim tale, unrelieved by any touches of humor. In it, Chayefsky seems to decry bitterly the total drabness of urban life in which baseball becomes a viable fantasy world. Edgar Castle's world gives him no sense of direction or purpose,

only a vague worship for success and a sense of shame at being a
blue-collar worker. More than in any of Chayefsky's other work, we
are confronted in this story with the dehumanized products of the
urban jungle. The only strong emotion we see is the impulse toward
meaningless violence, and we find a total lack of such qualities as
love, imagination, or will. Edgar Castle would fit perfectly in such
nightmare visions of urban life as Hubert Selby's *Last Exit to Brook-
lyn*.

Chayefsky's manner of narration is spare and unemotional, for his
style is that of the later Naturalists. There is no attempt to elicit
sympathy, only to present a case history the reader may take as
typical. If there is any weakness in the story, it is Chayefsky's failure
to present a clear scheme of causality. Could Edgar's failure be
traced to his ineffectual father who refuses to admit his son's inadequacies, or is it solely a function of the urban setting? Moreover,
Chayefsky is also terribly sloppy about chronology: the time scheme
is totally inconsistent, and the reader must go by Edgar's age and
not by the given dates. Still, the story presents Chayefsky's purest
response to his Naturalistic heritage, and it is also his only expression of unrelieved pessimism.

"Fifth from Garibaldi," "A Few Kind Words from Newark," and
"The Giant Fan" are clearly apprentice works by a man who was still
in the process of choosing his models and developing his own style.
They show the beginnings of a gifted writer, and they are interesting
in their relationship to Chayefsky's literary heritage. His best work,
however, was yet to come.

CHAPTER 2

The Bard of the Small Screen

IN the early 1950's, Chayefsky's career took a fortuitous turn when Arnold Shulman, a friend and radio writer, got him a job adapting scripts for "Theater Guild of the Air," a radio show that specialized in hour-long adaptations of stage successes. His first adaptation was George M. Cohan's *The Meanest Man in the World* for James Stewart and Josephine Hull, and this production was followed by "Tommy" and "Over 21." He also wrote for Dupont's series of documentary dramas, "Cavalcade of America." From radio, Chayefsky went to television; and he began writing scripts for half-hour live mysteries, *Danger* and *Manhunt*. His work for these shows caught the attention of David Susskind, producer of the "Philco Television Playhouse;" between the autumn of 1953 and May, 1955, Chayefsky had eleven scripts produced for this series. Only one of these eleven Chayefsky scripts was an adaptation, despite the fact that, as his friend, Mel Goldberg has commented, "Most of us were interested in doing adaptations — they were easy and you could knock them off fast and we all needed the money. But Paddy decided he couldn't do them. I'm sure he could have, but he felt he had things of his own to say and he didn't want to work with other people's material. It's always been much more important to him to be doing his own work, even at the expense of a buck. Paddy has an image of himself as a fine writer."[1] But television writing in the early days was, as now, hack work. Since the pay was not good, and since a writer survived by producing as many scripts as possible, he submitted a script, had it accepted, and then started another. Chayefsky worried more about his work, however, than about his income: and, as a result, he began a practice that shaped much of his career: "A writer must attend rehearsals for his own self-respect and because so much can be done."[2] Chayefsky insisted from the beginning on control of his material; and this protectiveness, which led to some friction and eventually to his own production company, had a crucial effect: Chayefsky gave the television and the film writer a stature he had not had before, and the result made the writer equal in status and in authority to the director and stars.

Bernard Kalb once described Paddy Chayefsky's television plays as being "as authentically Bronx as a rush hour subway bound for the Grand Concourse."[3] In today's less representational theater, this comment would hardly be considered the highest accolade, but in the mid-1950's, when Realism dominated the American theater and *Death of a Salesman* was considered "the great American play," such a testimony to an author's verisimilitude was high praise indeed. Chayefsky prides himself, above all, on his craftsmanship; and, shrewd artisan that he is, he began his career writing about what he knew best: the people of the city, not the glamorous city-dweller that Hollywood celebrated, but the typical urbanite who dwells in a homely walk-up on a crowded street. His subjects are the common frailties and problems of post-war urban America, and his theme is common to all his characters and situations: how does one give life meaning, or at least the illusion of meaning?

I   *The Television Writer*

The so-called "Golden Age of Television" seems like a rosy myth to those who were brought up in an age of situation comedies and ninety-minute, mini-epics ground out on Universal's back lot. It did exist, however, and it was exciting. Every network had at least one hour-long, weekly program that featured original drama and well-written adaptations of other works. Monday featured "Robert Montgomery Presents" and "Studio One"; Tuesday offered "The United States Steel Hour"; Wednesday, "Kraft Television Theater"; and "Armstrong Circle Theater"; Thursday, "Playhouse Ninety"; and Sunday, "Philco Television Playhouse." These programs spawned such acting talent as Paul Newman, JoAnne Woodward, Eva Marie Saint, Walter Matthau, and Martin Balsam; and they employed such writers as Rod Serling, Tad Mosel, Gore Vidal, and Stirling Silliphant. The plays were broadcast live, with all the attendant noise and technical awkwardness; but the actors and the excitement compensated for such handicaps. In this world, Paddy

Chayefsky not only flourished but received by 1955 such accolades as "television's best writer"[4] — a plaudit which in those days meant something; and he even had fan clubs organized among his admirers.

Chayefsky's triumph in television drama was the result of a perfect marriage of material and medium. A twelve-inch, black-and-white screen could not convey a large-scale drama effectively, nor could the exigencies of weekly television dramas allow large-scale productions. Plays could not demand extravagant or complex mounting, and intimacy became a virtue. Rod Serling, another noted television writer, wrote of the limitations imposed by television's "smallness": "You write 'big' for the movies. You let your camera tell considerably more story than you do in television. You write with a much more pronounced sense of physical action than you are permitted in the electronic medium. Television also demands a visual sense, but very often the progression of a story must be indicated by dialogue. In the movies it can be externalized just by what is seen and not necessarily by what is heard."[5] Tad Mosel, also a featured writer of teleplays, stressed the positive aspect of the medium's forced intimacy: "Never before has there been a medium so suited to what I call the 'personal drama' — that is, a play in which a writer explores one simple happening, a day, or even an hour, and tries to suggest a complete life."[6]

In the early days of television, the audience was basically urban and middle class. This type of audience has always responded well to two types of theater — the escapist show that would allow them temporary relief from their problems, and the play that spoke simply and sympathetically about their lives. Chayefsky's interest in depicting realistically "the people I understand; the $75 to $125 a week people,"[7] and his belief in small-scale, focused plays made him an excellent match for his medium and his audience. Moreover, another important dimension of Chayefsky's work augured well for its success: his limitation of the scope of narrative. Chayefsky's connecting essays in the edition of his television plays demonstrate his understanding of and sympathy with the pressures and demands that are peculiar to writing for television. He knew that he had to tell a story effectively in fifty-three minutes and that this fact necessitated a simple structure: "I have only one rule that I consider absolute and arbitrary, and that is: a drama can have only one story.

It can have only one leading character. All other stories and all other characters are used in the script only as they facilitate the main story."[8]

Chayefsky began writing his plays by conceiving a motive situation which is usually the climactic scene. He then decided what was necessary to lead to that scene and how the crisis could be resolved most effectively: "Dramatic construction, as far as I am concerned, is essentially a search for reasons. That is to say, given the second act curtain incident, construction consists of finding reasons why the characters involved in the incident act as they do. . . . No matter how the writer approaches the construction of his script, it always comes down to justifying his moment of crisis, and this is what I call the search for reasons" (82).

Chayefsky's comments about writing for television sound very much like Eugène Scribe describing his Well-Made Plays, and such echoes hardly sound praiseworthy in the post-Ibsen era. Yet, as Scribe in the nineteenth century was trying to develop principles for writing within the new framework of a theater that demanded a semblance of verisimilitude, so Chayefsky was attempting to communicate the mechanics of writing for a new dramatic medium that imposed severe limitations of time and focus. Like Scribe, his comments are those of a craftsman rather than of a visionary.

II Chayefsky's Method

A close look at one of Chayefsky's lesser television scripts, "Printer's Measure," shows much about the writer's method. Commenting on "Printer's Measure" in the published volume of television plays, Chayefsky demonstrates precisely how the play was constructed. It began with an idea: an old printer slaps a young boy who works in his shop because the boy is going to train himself to run a linotype machine, anathema to the old craftsman. The setting — an old print shop — is picturesque; and the story reflects the age-old conflict between the old order of craftsmanship and the new order of technological efficiency. In order to make that climactic slap dramatically effective, the writer has to develop the relationship of the old man and the boy; but the old man must be shown to be fond enough of the boy for his "defection" to hurt him; the young boy, to be a sympathetic character, must have reasons for joining the enemy — the forces of progress. Therefore, the scenes leading to the climax must develop not only the central relationship but also a situation that explains the young man's desire to become a linotype operator. The reason is money, and the motive impulse is the death of the boy's father. Moreover, the linotype machine must be established as a threat to the old man's job as well as to his philosophy if the audience is to sympathize with his strong reaction.

All this preparation has to be accomplished in thirty-six minutes in order to prepare for the slap that closes the second act. With such a stringent time limit, the writer must plan quite methodically; and he must also keep in mind that he is going to be able to do little more in such a short time than develop the major relationship between the old man and the boy. Any additional characters are merely going to be pawns to develop this line of action: ". . . the character traits that go into the various characterizations are likewise contrived solely to satisfy the demands of the main character's story. It is a common illusion that dramatists sit down and preconceive a detailed biography and character study of each character in the script. To a professional writer, this would be a palpable waste of time" (86). To an idealistic playwright, this acceptance of arbitrary rules might seem a bit crass; but Chayefsky, like any effective artist, believes that a good writer masters the form he is given. The result of Chayefsky's careful planning is a play in which the conflicts are touchingly embodied in two very successful characters.

Mr. Healy, the old Irish typesetter of "Printer's Measure," is an old man in the midst of a crisis. Like the artisans of his generation, he takes great pride in his craft and in its tradition; and he feels only disdain for the less personal modern methods represented by the new linotype that his boss has brought into the shop. Since the linotype is also part of the new technology that has displaced the old artisans regardless of their skill, Mr. Healy, a stubborn, temperamental old man, takes the intrusion of the linotype so strongly that he tries to destroy the machine with a sledge hammer. The foil to Mr. Healy is the linotype operator who is cold and efficient; he is concerned not with pride in his work but with his efficiency and his income. The young apprentice in the shop, in need of a good income to help support his widowed mother and his college-bound sister, must choose between the joy and pride of good craftsmanship and the high salary afforded by becoming an extension of the linotype machine. In choosing the latter, he offers the telling blow to the old man.

Like many men his age, Healy will not retire, for his identity is totally defined by his work: "That's my trade, man! That's my trade! I'd crumble into my coffin without my trade" (55). His work gives his life meaning, and he sees the machine as a threat to the dignity of all working men:

A man's work is the sweetest thing he owns. It would do us a lot better to invent some labor-making devices. We've gone mad, boy, with this mad chase for comfort, and it's sure we're losing the very juice of living. It's a sad business, boy, when they sit a row of printers down in a line, and the machine clacks, and the mats flip, and when it comes out, the printer has about as much joy of creation as the delivery boy. There's no joy in this kind of life, boy — no joy. It's a very hard hundred dollars a week, I'll tell you that! (77)

In his comments, Chayefsky refers to "Printer's Measure" as "a good, sound piece of theater, probably the best-constructed script in the book" (81). Certainly the play embraces more separate, yet interrelated scenes than most; and it also has a theme that raises the piece above the specific. Mr. Healy's war with the machine says much about our country's rush toward a technological society after World War II and about the price the working man has paid for this "brave new world." Moreover, the play is enriched by having two central characters; for the boy's dilemma also engages our sympathies. It is his mother's dream that his sister should go to college, but the boy must provide the money that will make that dream come true. The thought of sacrificing so much of himself so that his sister can go to college, instead of finding a husband to support her, is not a pleasant one; but, for his mother, it is a crucial part of a changing world that a woman should be able to follow her ambition: "But the world is changing, and, if a woman's got a spark, it's her right and privilege to make a thing of herself. It's like this old friend of yours in the shop. The machine is there, but he won't accept it. . . . If we cannot hold on to old things, we must make peace with the new. Your sister has a talent. You had best make peace with that, Tom" (66). Because of his sister's education, Tom betrays his old friend and goes to linotype school. Like most people, Tom cannot afford the luxury of following the old ways.

Despite his concern for maintaining focus, Chayefsky's plays have been justly celebrated for his ability to include those details of setting and characterization that make a play convincing. We get to know the printer through his conversations with his old friends and with his family, interchanges that are, of necessity, brief, but very telling. We see the boy's resentment of his sister's college education and his mother's strong desire for her daughter to have the opportunities she was denied. Chayefsky also gives us a vivid picture of the printer's boss, a man torn between his loyalty and affection for the old printer and his desire to keep abreast of his competitors. Characteristically, Chayefsky sharpens these brief moments with extremely accurate renderings of the rhythms of speech of his characters. Set against the garrulous talk of the old workmen complaining about the inroads of technology — language with the coloring of the Old World from which these men came — is the brash, laconic language of the followers of progress: "I made as high as hundred fifty. I once worked for a couple of guys on Broadway and Twenty-fifth. They had four linotypes and a proof press. They were racking in easy two, three hundred bucks apiece every week" (67). All these elements are contained within a fifty-three minute play that seems to be simplicity itself.

The key to mastering a medium is not only the craftsman's knowledge of how to master its limitations; it also entails understanding the medium's greatest potential. Chayefsky's success is based greatly on his understanding of what television drama could achieve most effectively: "Now, the word for television drama is depth, the digging under the surface of life for the more profound truths of human relationships. This is an area that no other dramatic medium has handled or can adequately handle" (132). Chayefsky's plays, then, would, through careful rendering of character and milieu, explore what lies underneath a relationship. These relationships would not be tested by profound crises but by the sort of problems that affect most people: "Television is better suited to everyday crises, through which the same depth of insight can be achieved, but without the excessive theatricality" (127). The conflict between an old printer and his young assistant might not be material for scaling Sophoclean heights, but it does reflect effectively some real problems that members of Chayefsky's audience face in some form or another. The result is an effective, intimate drama with which the audience can readily identify.

Part of the strong sense of identification on the part of the audience is due to the author's own identification with his material; and Chayefsky, always a thorough researcher of setting and background, prefers to write out of personal experience. In the case of "Printer's Measure," Chayefsky worked for years in his uncle's print shop; and his brother, Winn, operates a commercial printing plant. Chayefsky's interest in this setting and subject is documented by an early story about the suicide of a bankrupt printer while his equipment is being auctioned off. The story, like the later play, is heightened by the sense of reality that Chayefsky's experience gives it. This sense of reality was crucial to a writer who saw television's sense of realism as its chief virtue: "Realism, in the theatre, is a synthesized business; what one achieves is really the effect of realism. In television you can be literally and freely real. The scenes can be played as if the actors were unaware of their audience. The dialogue can sound as if it had been wire-tapped."[9]

The fruits of Chayefsky's mastery of television drama made him a household word and gave him a celebrity accorded few writers in any medium. More noteworthy is the fact that these plays are moving reading twenty years after their first appearance on television. If time is the ultimate test of the artistic merit of a work, then most of the eleven plays Chayefsky wrote for "Philco Television Playhouse" have proven their worth. Eleven plays, however, is a small output for that time; the reason is difficult to determine. Rumors were spread, however, that after Chayefsky's success with the film adaptation of *Marty* he had priced himself out of the market. In a medium that does not place a high value on good dramatic writing, paying a substantial fee for an established writer may not have seemed a necessary investment. Moreover, despite Chayefsky's success with the public and the sponsors, comtemporary releases in the trade papers suggest that the sponsors did not think Chayefsky's commonplace Realism offered the best showcase for tires and for television sets in elegant cabinets.

Fortunately, six of the Philco plays were published by Simon and Schuster. Continued interest in these fine works has kept the volume in print for almost two decades. The volume, *Television Plays*, does not contain "Middle of the Night," which was later published in its Broadway version (see Chapter 3), "A Catered Affair," "The Sixth Year," "The Reluctant Citizen," or "Catch My Boy on Sunday." We might quibble about some of the choices of plays for the collection, but Chayefsky's volume is as much a vehicle for his lengthy and illuminating discussions of television drama as it is for a collection of his plays. For his discussion, some of the lesser known plays served most effectively. Though I will discuss all the plays except "Middle of the Night," the four most successful plays in the published collection, plays considered among the best television has offered, are "The Big Deal," "Marty," "The Mother," and "The Bachelor Party."

III *Early Teleplays: The Old World in the New*

Chayefsky's first three plays for the "Philco Television Playhouse" — "Holiday Song," "The Reluctant Citizen," and "Printer's Measure" — have much in common; for each deals with an old man's problem in reconciling his traditional views with the confusion of mid-century urban life. Two of the three, "The Reluctant Citizen" and "Holiday Song," have a distinctly ethnic flavor; all three mix a serious situation with warm humor.

"Holiday Song," Chayefsky's first hour-long script, is an adaptation of a *Readers' Digest* story, one of those simple anecdotes that are a traditional part of the publication, about a photographer, a Hungarian immigrant, who changed his usual pattern one day and took a different subway. On the train, he found himself next to another Hungarian man, a victim of the concentration camps, who had lost track of his wife and had given her up for dead. The photographer had recently met on the subway a Hungarian woman who met the man's description of his wife; he went on to locate this woman and affected a husband-wife reunion that affirmed his belief in a benevolent God. The story is a simple one, perhaps too simple for an hour-long play; but it is fascinating to observe how Chayefsky fleshes out this bare outline. His central character is not just a photographer but a cantor, a man of God who has, through observing the cruelty and inhumanity around him, lost his faith: ". . . it was like I went to bed one night, and I woke up the next morning — and I was thinking: What sadness in this world! I seem to hear nothing or see nothing but sadness. And at night, I would hear in my head like a drum — God-God-God. What sort of a God is it would allow this?" (8). Although the day of the action is Rosh Hashanah, and although the cantor is needed for the evening service, his new skepticism makes his religious work impossible. In fact, he refuses to let his niece marry the man who wants to marry her. The suitor is a devout Jew, but the cantor fears his own faithlessness makes her marriage impossible. Chayefsky creates a religious-domestic crisis as the background for the "miracle" on the subway. The interest is not so much in the plot as it is in the central character — the serious, lovable old man who is overwhelmed by his sudden loss of faith. The setting, his Long Island home, kept by his niece, provides that mixture of the mundane and the spiritual that later made *The Tenth Man* such a success. The first shot is of the cantor's robes on an ironing board, and the play's flavor is created by the simple dialogue of the carefully depicted group of characters. The old Jew, in Old World style, not only expects his daughter to wait on him but also turns every subject into a religious disputation; and the women worry about making a good marriage for the young niece and about providing a fitting feast for the high holiday.

The cantor is sent to visit the wise Rabbi Marcus to discuss his loss of faith; but, when he reaches the subway station at which he must change trains for Manhattan, a guard directs him to the wrong train; and on it he meets the sobbing woman who thinks she has lost her husband in a concentration camp. Meeting this sad victim of man's cruelty only serves to affirm the cantor's new-found skepticism: "The same sadness. Everywhere I look, the same sadness. . . . Dear, dear young lady — there is no God!" (13). When the cantor is sent back to Rabbi Marcus, he is again directed to the wrong train by a guard; and he meets this time the husband of the unfortunate woman and brings the couple together. Upon returning to the transfer point, he discovers that the guard who directed him to the wrong trains was not a subway guard, but an agent of God: "And ye shall know Him in the strangest costumes and in the strangest places" (34). The cantor's faith is reaffirmed and all is well.

I recount this story in detail to demonstrate the ways in which Chayefsky has turned an all-too-simple coincidence into a touching play. The most crucial addition is "color," the kind that comes from the carefully detailed presentation of characters who typify a way of life. There is no great intellectual substance here, and the "message" that was at the center of the original story is now the denouement of an effective drama. We may quibble about the need for the niece's awkward courtship with the jeweler from Cleveland, but it presents another aspect of the world Chayefsky is depicting, a touching detail in a larger painting. Indeed, Chayefsky, when he wrote this script, ". . . was governed by an almost compulsive interest in Jewish folklore and humor. I had been wanting to write a show about synagogue life for years" (37). This same interest was to be an integral part of his conception of his first original stage play, *The Tenth Man*.

Old Mr. Kimmer, the central character of "The Reluctant Citizen," has a less spiritual problem. A new arrival in America in 1946 after years of cruel handling by the Nazis, Kimmer lives in fear of everyone. Though he wants to become an American citizen, everyone in authority is a source of such terror that he finds himself incapable of communicating; but the play ends, of course, with the old man's taking the oath of allegiance. The central setting of "The Reluctant Citizen" is the Educational Alliance on the Lower East Side of New York. The Alliance served as an education and orientation center for immigrants, particularly Jewish ones; and through the eyes of the workers at the Alliance, we see that Mr. Kimmer's problem is not unique among those visiting there. After years of persecution, he lives in fear; as an old man, he has lost faith in his ability to accomplish anything significant; but the Alliance, much more than Kimmer's loving family, gives the old man a new faith in himself.

"The Reluctant Citizen" demonstrates Chayefsky's ability to take a simple situation and enrich it with local color and authentic language. The audience's interest in this simple tale is sustained not only by the picture of the Kimmer family making a new life in America while remembering lovingly their life in the Old World, but by the crusty old people at the Alliance and by the dedicated but discouraged social workers: "I've got all these old people, and I want them to realize what rich lives they have! I want them to learn they don't have to depend on their children! That they don't have to be afraid of being old! That they can be useful and productive citizens! But I can't get to them!"[10]

No doubt the documentary flavor of this early play was influenced by Chayefsky's experience with the "Cavalcade of America," a documentary series on radio for which he wrote two episodes. This sense of realism is enhanced by Chayefsky's characteristic attention to detail — the description of the luxury of white bread in the old country and the dialogue of the old people in the craft workshop —

which gives his work much of its charm. Despite its signs of Chayefsky's promise as a playwright, "The Reluctant Citizen" lacks focus. Chayefsky attempts not only to tell Mr. Kimmer's story but also something about the attitudes of his family and the work of the Educational Alliance. The point of view is split between Kimmer and the zealous young social worker, and such a dual focus weakens the short teleplay.

"Holiday Song" and "The Reluctant Citizen," with "Printer's Measure," form something of a trilogy. Their theme is the conflict between the traditional society of the Old World and the New World of technology and the modern city. Through these plays, we see the old faith affirmed in the face of urban chaos; human love and compassion affirmed despite memories of human cruelty; and the pride of human work affirmed despite the necessity of technology in a modern society. Chayefsky's three old men are transition figures who are the products of a simpler age but who have to live in post-war America. How much of the positive aspects of the Old World will their children keep in the face of America's worship of progress and her lack of respect for tradition? In his next four plays, Chayefsky focuses on these children and on their lives in the New World.

IV   *"The Big Deal"*

"The Big Deal," while containing an effective character study, demonstrates how a writer can be trapped by attempting a subject too complex for the time allotted; for this play moves effectively to its crisis while speeding to its denouement with too many untied ends. Joe Manx, the central character is another version of one of America's archetypal characters — the operator who "made it big," who lost it, but who cannot surrender his dream of "making it" again. Manx was a successful building speculator in Toledo twenty years ago; but, since some lean years and some bad gambles decimated his fortune, he is now supported for the most part by his young daughter. Joe has the opportunity to take a civil service job for which he is highly qualified — that of a building inspector — with a modest annual salary; but such a job is not big enough for Joe Manx. He wants to try again for the big fortune by buying some swampland and converting it into a housing development. When none of his former associates will loan him the money to buy the land, he turns to his daughter and asks her to loan him the money that she has saved to help support her and her future husband while he finishes medical school. Touched by her loving willingness to sacrifice her future for his and overcome by remorse at his selfishness, Joe refuses the loan and takes the civil service job.

There are two sides to Chayefsky's Joe Manx: the selfish dreamer and the generous man. Totally unrealistic, he sees himself as "a big shot." He fails to see that the world has passed him by and that his schemes are impractical: "Four lousy thousand bucks! You can't lend me four lousy thousand bucks! What am I, some kind of a bum or something? I built plenty of houses in my time! Good double-brick houses, three coats of plaster!" (117). Joe's dreams not only keep him from helping his family in any practical way but also motivate his using its money. When we first meet him, he is borrowing money from his daughter so that he can impress an old associate by taking him to lunch; later, he is willing to gamble his daughter's future on a few acres of swampland.

What makes this character more than a stereotype is the fact that Joe Manx is loved by those closest to him; for, beneath his deluded and selfish ambition, he is a generous man who feels that he has failed his family: "You talk about facing facts! All right, let's face some facts! I failed as a man! I failed as a father! What did I ever give these two women?! What did I ever give them?! My wife wears the same cloth coat for four years, do you know that?!" (119). It is the inadequacy brought on by fifteen years of bankruptcy that Joe Manx wants to wipe out with his big deal. What he does not realize is that his wife and daughter love him regardless of his failure in the business world. His wife tells him: "Joe, we don't want a million dollars from you. We love you, Joe, we love you if you build houses or if you don't build houses. We just want to have you around the house. We like to eat dinner with you. We like to see your face" (122). When his daughter Marilyn unquestioningly offers her savings, Joe breaks down with remorse:

JOE: (*brokenly*) What did I ever give you?

He sinks down into a chair, cupping his face in both hands now. The daughter moves slowly to him.

DAUGHTER: Pa, look at me. Am I an unhappy girl? I'm happy. I love
          George. I love you. I love Mama. I got a responsible job. The
          boss is satisfied with me. That's what you gave me. I'll make
          you out the check. (125)

We cannot help but think that the audience needs more information in order to accept the wife's and the daughter's loving views
about Joe. All we have seen is an unhappy deluded man who will
sacrifice his family to his dream of winning a "big deal." He has been
bankrupt for fifteen years, and he has offered his family little but his
promises about the future success and his memories of his past
affluence. We are told by his family that he is a loving man, but this
side of Joe needs to be developed more fully before we can sympathize with him as we should. Nor does it seem likely that his
fifteen years of dreaming would be erased by one simple act of love.
One doubts that a middle-aged man could change so suddenly.
Essentially, we are given a strong impression not of Joe's love for his
wife and daughter, but of their unyielding devotion to him. They
love him in spite of his indifference toward them. It would take
more time, however, than Chayefsky had at his disposal to establish
that side of Joe that elicits the love of his family.

The most effective scenes in "The Big Deal" are those outside the
family. Joe's attempts to get support from his friends, his fanatical
will to emulate their success, his inability to accept his own
position — these are the convincing aspects of Joe's personality.
Most successful is the poker game at Harry Gerber's house where
Joe's ambition is contrasted to the complacency of his successful
friends. Joe breaks down at their realistic indifference toward his
scheme, but we see all too clearly through Joe's friends that the
attainment of Joe's dream of success is much less exciting than the
dream itself. Their success has not given these men any magnificent
changes in their lives; therefore, to them, the magic Joe is seeking
just doesn't exist, and the power that comes with success only brings
headaches and ulcers.

The characters are brought to life through the sense of reality
imparted by the dialogue. Chayefsky delineates Joe through his
breathless, feverish language: "I went to them all, Harry. I went to
Daugherty, to Shirmer. I went to Sam Harvard, Marty Kingsley,
Irving Stone. Some of these men used to mix cement for me. I
couldn't raise four thousand dollars! Daugherty brushed me off like I
was mud on his pants. . . . What does it mean? What does it mean?"

(118). Joe's tense language is set against the calm, self-satisfied sound of the other men: "Oh, land. Land I don't know anything about. If you were in some kind of trouble — if you needed an operation or if you wanted to pay off a mortgage, something like that, I might be able to dig up a couple of thousand for you. But land I'm not interested in . . . (116–17). Or we have the logical concern of his wife: "I think something terrible is going to happen to him. He doesn't talk like a completely sensible person any more. I look at him sometimes; it seems to me he's in another world, dreaming" (110).

Chayefsky's ear for dialogue is particularly keen in recording the inflections of second-generation Americans, speech patterns that contain some of the accents and syntax of their European origin: "So, Joe, this suit, rain or shine, it holds its crease. It doesn't wrinkle. I could jump in the river and swim in it, it won't wrinkle. The only trouble is, it makes me sweat so much. I'll be honest with you. I don't know how they manage in Egypt with it" (116). Moreover, the contrasting rhythms of the dialogue give Chayefsky's television plays their pace far more than the actors or the director. Nonetheless, his dialogue carries with it a limitation that has an adverse effect on "The Big Deal" because it is that which is primarily associated with New Yorkers. "The Big Deal" may nominally take place in Toledo, Ohio, but its language has none of the flavor of the Midwest. Joe Manx and his friends are misplaced New Yorkers, and the locale of this play is that of its language and not that of its setting. But "The Big Deal" is a play that is a success despite its flaws. The resolution may be too facile, but Joe and his friends give the play such life that we are interested spectators.

V *"The Mother"*

"The Mother" is, on the other hand, an almost perfectly wrought little play. The two principal characters are convincingly suggested and the primary relationship well conceived. In contrast to Joe Manx, who is financially dependent on his daughter, the recently widowed Mrs. Fanning is fighting for her independence. She wants to be beholden to no one but finds many obstacles to attaining self-sufficiency. Mrs. Fanning has always been a housewife; and with the death of her husband, she must find useful work, but her lack of skill is a handicap. Her one day behind a sewing machine in a clothing factory is disastrous as her lack of the necessary dexterity and her physical frailty manifest themselves. The worst obstacle to independence, however, is her younger daughter Annie who needs desperately to have her mother dependent upon her. Because of her own sense of inadequacy and guilt, Annie can't bear to see her mother living alone. She puts the needs of her own family behind her sense of responsibility to her mother, not realizing that her mother needs a sense of independence to survive. Annie's sister says, "You can't tell Annie nothing. Annie was born at a wrong time. The doctor told my mother she was gonna die if she had Annie, and my mother has been scared of Annie ever since. And if Annie thinks she's going to get my mother to love her with all these sacrifices, she's crazy. . . . She's doing the worst thing for my mother, absolutely the worst thing" (205). If her mother can come into her household, perhaps Annie will have the attention from her that she has never had.

When Mrs. Fanning returns from her first and last day at the clothing factory, she finds her loneliness and sense of failure unbearable; and, after calling her other children and finding them busy, she calls Annie and asks her if she might spend the night at her house. Annie happily accepts and has her husband pick her mother up and bring her to the house. After one night, however, the mother decides to go back to her apartment: "I'm a woman of respect. I can take care of myself. I always have. And don't tell me it's raining because it stopped about an hour ago. And don't say you'll drive me home because I can get the bus two blocks away. Work is the meaning of my life. It's all I know what to do. I can't change my ways at this late time" (218). When the mother leaves, Annie finally accepts her primary responsibility to her husband and family.

Chayefsky gives this timely story emotive force by creating a succession of scenes that show the lives of so many old people; for their grown children are either over-solicitous or wholly concerned with their own lives and their contemporaries live a cycle of television and meaningless banter on the park bench. As one older adult explains, "There's ever so much fun on television in the afternoons, with the kiddie shows and a lot of dancing and Kate Smith and shows like that. But my daughter-in-law's cleaning up today, and she doesn't like me around the house when she's cleaning, so I came out a bit early to sit in the park" (193). In quick brush strokes, Chayefsky delineates the plight of the aged — victims of lack of respect, they have a feeling of uselessness and meaninglessness such as the one that Mrs. Fanning fights. She may be welcome in Annie's home, but she would be another child and all too obviously a burden; to maintain any dignity, she must be independent. The play is enriched, too, by the characterization of Annie who is still trying to establish a meaningful relationship with her mother at any price. Annie only sees in her mother what she needs from her, and her desire for her mother's attention blinds her to the needs of her own family.

The little details, too, give the play its richness; and an example is the scene in the mother's apartment in which the daughter will not let her mother fix her own coffee:

OLD LADY: Annie, you know, you can drive somebody crazy, do you know that?

DAUGHTER: I can drive somebody crazy? *You're* the one who can drive somebody crazy.

OLD LADY: Will you stop hovering over me like I was a cripple in a wheel chair. I can make my own coffee, believe me. Why did you come over here? You've got a husband and two kids to take care of. Go make coffee for them, for heaven's sakes. (187)

Chayefsky clearly understands, as does Mrs. Fanning, that her fight for independence may be a futile one at this stage of her life, but without it she is dead. He also understands — and here is one key to his success — that small incidents can tell a great deal about human relationships, just as this scene about coffee-making establishes the central mother-daughter relationship.

Within its limited scope, "The Mother" is a fine play. Its two major characters are fully drawn, the supporting characters are well conceived and fulfill their functions successfully, and the many short scenes are well unified into a convincing picture of two people in an all-too-typical dilemma.

VI   "Marty"

"Marty" is, no doubt, Paddy Chayefsky's most famous work not only because of its highly successful television appearance that was directed, as were most of Chayefsky's plays, by Delbert Mann and that starred Rod Steiger and Betsy Palmer, but also because of its Academy Award-winning film realization with Ernest Borgnine and Betsy Blair (see Chapter IV). Indeed, "Marty" provided one of the classics of both television and the American film because it captures vividly and touchingly a number of aspects of the American experience. While being about people who are far from glamorous, its mundane characters have a beauty and a dignity that were felt by viewers far from the Bronx.

Marty Pilletti is a fat, thirty-six-year-old butcher whose sense of inadequacy because of his homeliness has kept him from establishing any meaningful relationship with a woman. He lives with his mother, and he spends his evenings with his friend, Angelo, in adolescent, futile searches for a good time. Their spare time is spent in a bar deciding the fateful question: "Well, what do you feel like doing tonight?" (137). If the answer is calling up a "girl," Marty protests:

Angie, I'm thirty-six years old, I been looking for a girl every Saturday night of my life. I'm a little short, fat, fellow, and girls don't go for me, that's all. I'm not like you. I mean, you joke around, and they laugh at you, and you get along fine. I just stand around like a bug. What's the sense of kidding myself? Everybody's always telling me to get married. Get married. Get married. Don't you think I wanna get married? I wanna get married. They drive me crazy. Now, I don't wanna wreck your Saturday night for you, Angie. You wanna go somewhere, you go ahead. I don't wanna go. (138)

After some pressure from his mother, Marty goes to a dance hall with Angelo where he meets Clara Davis, "a dog" who has been "ditched" by her date for a more attractive woman. Marty consoles Clara, and they share their hurts and their needs for a sense of worth in a world in which looks count far too much: "So it don't matter if you look like a gorilla. So you see, dogs like us, we ain't such dogs as we think we are" (158).

While Marty is at the dance hall, his mother has gone to bring her sister from the sister's son's home. The daughter-in-law has not been able to live with her husband's mother in the house, but the mother-in-law feels wounded at losing her Old World place in her son's home. She shares her fears with Marty's mother: "What will you do if Marty gets married?! What will you cook?! What happen to alla children tumbling in alla rooms?! Where is the noise! It is curse to be a widow!" (156). With these aroused fears, Marty's mother goes home to hear Marty's new girl say that "I don't think a mother-in-law should live with a young couple" (163).

After meeting a girl he really likes, a girl with whom he feels he can share his life, Marty finds his relationship with Clara threatened on all sides. His mother is threatened by this college graduate's alien ideas and by her non-Italian origins; and his friends, who call her "a dog," keep him from calling her again. Finally, Marty asserts his will: "You don't like her. My mother don't like her. She's a dog and I'm a fat, ugly little man. All I know is I had a good time last night. I'm gonna have a good time tonight. If we have enough good times together, I'm going down on my knees and beg that girl to marry me" (172).

What is most extraordinary about "Marty" is the amount of material Chayefsky can include in less than an hour. We have not only Marty's bourgeoning relationship with Clara but also those with his family and with his friends. We see Marty in all his roles: first, as butcher; second, as an aging adolescent with his aimless friends; third, as a son and a brother; and, fourth, as man in love. The last view gives a meaning to his life that allows him to see the other roles in their proper perspective: he must be the man of his own house, and he cannot live meaningfully by wandering around with Angelo every night. In his comments, Chayefsky rather pretentiously but accurately writes that, ". . . in *Marty*, I ventured lightly into such values as the Oedipal relationship, the reversion to adolescence by many 'normal' Americans, and the latent homosexuality of the middle class" (174) — and he accomplished these objectives in fifty-three minutes. What might be more accurately said is that Marty's problem is that his feelings of inadequacy keep him in an immature relationship with his mother and in an adolescent relationship with his friend, Angelo. Since his feelings about himself keep him a child, only love for a woman, a wife, can free him from his self-concern.

Another conflict in "Marty" that is crucial to our understanding of Marty's plight is his being halfway between the Old World and the New. He has been reared in America by Italian parents who have ingrained in him the customs and mores of Italy. He is waited on by his mother as an Italian man would expect to be by a woman, but he falls in love with non-Italian, Clara, who has less traditional ideas. The conflict between the two sets of values is dramatized vividly by the direct juxtaposition of Marty's first meeting with Clara and the conversation between his mother and his aunt. While Marty finds the person who will give his life meaning, his aunt bemoans the loss of her traditional position in her son's house because of tension that exists between her and her daughter-in-law. This scene establishes the potential conflict between Marty's mother and Clara, a conflict that is economically developed later; but it also presents Marty's inevitable conflict with the values of Italian tradition as expressed by his aunt: "This is my son's house. This is where I live" (155). Other aspects of this awkward combination of Italy and the Bronx appear in the final scene that takes place at the traditional gathering of the men in a tavern after church. By marrying "the dog," a non-Italian one at that, Marty will no longer be at home in this world.

Throughout "Marty," Chayefsky also vividly suggests a series of tense relationships between the sexes. Men look at women in the most immature ways — as mothers or as mindless ornaments; but, though Marty may be nominal head of his household, his mother is clearly in charge. Marty's brother, Thomas, has traded a shrewish mother for a shrewish, overbearing wife. Outside the home, the men talk only about female bodies; and even Marty, after meeting Clara, awkwardly grabs for a kiss like a teenager in a back seat. This picture of extended adolescence is not presented satirically but as a given, a crucial aspect of Marty's world. Indeed, one of Chayefsky's gifts is the ability to make his audience suspend judgment about his characters. He wants our sympathy and understanding. Perhaps, this relationship between audience and material makes Chayefsky so successful a television writer: he brings other homes into those of his viewers. The relationship between viewer and play becomes as intimate as the domestic setting in which the play is viewed.

"Marty" 's success is also attributable to Chayefsky's fortunate reluctance to resolve all the conflicts he has developed at the end of the play. Marty may have decided to call Clara despite his friends' and his mother's opinion of her, but that only means that he will confront the inevitable conflicts rather than avoid them by remaining a thirty-six-year-old adolescent. The end of the play is really, therefore, only the beginning of more but different conflicts for Marty.

VII   *"The Bachelor Party"*

"The Bachelor Party," which was also adapted into a film, remains more effective in its shorter version for television. The play is, essentially, a development of a theme suggested in "Marty" — the inability of many middle-class American men to accept the mature roles of husband and father and their attempts, therefore, to prolong their adolescence. Moreover, this problem is presented in a milieu in which no alternative seems particularly meaningful. Charlie, a bookkeeper in a New York office, lives with his wife, Helen, in a small low-rent apartment in Jersey City; and his life seems little more than his office, his apartment, and the Hudson-Manhattan Subway. Charlie is restless, and his feeling of entrapment is reinforced by the news of his wife's pregnancy:

It seems to me I got one crummy life ahead of me. It just seems like I go to my job every day, and I come home, and we eat dinner, and then we go see Helen's mother and father or my mother and father. Or my cousin Julie and her husband. And now we got this kid coming. That's what the rest of my life is going to be like. I'm going to be a bookkeeper for seventy-two bucks a week the rest of my life. I don't know. Sometimes, I look at Helen. And she's a nice girl and all that. She's pretty. But I feel I'm missing something. I look at Helen. I say: I must have felt something special to marry this girl. Something beautiful, you know what I mean? I mean, I love her, and all that, but . . . what's love? (228–29)

During the course of a long, disillusioning evening, Charlie finds the answer to his question. The occasion is a bachelor party for one of Charlie's co-workers, Arnold; and it is the customary "last night of freedom" for the prospective groom. The host is Eddie, the "swinging" bachelor and the envy of the married men in the office because his life seems to them to be a round of women, parties, and nice cars. What the men finally realize during the evening is that Eddie's frantic attempts to keep the party going from bar to bar are made to keep from being alone because his life is emptier than theirs: no one shares it. Yet, the party is an attempt on the part of Charlie and his friends to share the freedom they think Eddie has. In reality, the party is a regression because the attendants sing high school songs and look for girls.

This attempt to regain the freedom of adolescence is darkened by the expressions of entrapment on the part of the husbands and the groom's growing fear of his forthcoming marriage: "What am I going to do with her, Charlie. She's one of those quiet ones. I'm not much of a talker myself. What are me and this girl going to do, just sit there, nobody talking" (247). Arnold's fears grow to the breaking point; and, lubricated by liquor, he calls his fiancée and cancels the engagement. Arnold's action and Eddie's insistence on keeping everybody together lead Charlie to see this bachelor party for what it is: "This is just what we used to do before I got married. The whole bunch of us would wander around the streets, making cracks at girls, then we'd wind up in a bar, drinking beer and yelling at each other. . . . We were looking, always looking for something. That's what we've been doing all night tonight. Going from one place to another, looking. What are we looking for?" (253).

When Charlie takes Arnold home, he tells Arnold why he shouldn't cancel his engagement; and he himself recognizes why his marriage is not a trap but a comfort: "That's what a wife's for. To make you feel you don't have to be ashamed of yourself. Then she tells you what makes her feel miserable. . . . Then, that's your job. It's your job to make her feel she's not as bad as everybody makes her think she is. That's what marriage is, Arnold. It's a job. You work at it. You work at it twenty-four hours a day. It's your job to make that person feel happy . . . but that's what my wife does for me. She's the one that makes life worth living" (256). The bachelor party is over, and Charlie can return to his life with some satisfaction.

"The Bachelor Party" is not a happy play because Chayefsky never sees life as more than a compromise with threatening forces within and without. No great joys exist in the life of a Bronx butcher or a Jersey City bookkeeper, and no spiritual insights make life golden. Urban life is tedious, and people in the lower middle class cannot break from the routine that determines their lives. The saving experience is love, not overwhelming passion nor ennobling romance, but the simple yet difficult love of two people who are willing to share each others lives. That love will remove no obstacles — it may create new ones — but it makes life possible. Chayefsky has made his play somewhat unrealistic by giving Charlie an ideal wife, totally devoted and totally sympathetic with Charlie's restlessness and disappointment at the imminent birth of their child. Helen can offer Charlie the solace he needs, yet Charlie's restlessness is also understandable: he suffers from one of the greatest fears of American men—the fear of a lifetime of sameness. We wonder with Charlie, as we do with Joe Manx, whether love conquers all as easily as Chayefsky seems to think it does.

Again, in a small scope, Chayefsky has given us a number of stories against which we see Charlie's. We have Eddie the bachelor, envied by his friends, but really a lonely man. Eddie constantly belittles marriage, but he has found no viable substitute. Kenneth, Charlie's subway companion, lives with memories of teenage escapades and with fantasies about the ladies on the subway. Arnold is terrified of a marriage with a woman he feels he barely knows. These are vignettes, but they avoid stereotype because they have the sting of familiarity. These simple character sketches are full enough for the viewer to identify them with people in similar situations — and with himself.

VIII *Three Mothers*

Not all of Chayefsky's plays display the technical mastery seen in the works discussed so far, and the principal problem is a lack of focus that fragments his lesser work. By the end of his television career, Chayefsky was obviously chafing at the bit of fifty-three minute vignettes and was beginning to break his own cardinal rule that a television play had only time for one story and one principal character. In his later teleplays, the distinction between background and foreground tends to break down; and "The Catered Affair," "The Sixth Year," and "Catch My Boy on Sunday" are weaker developments of earlier themes. All three plays deal with a middle-aged woman's lack of love for her husband and with the effect it has on her relationship with her child. At the center of each play is a failed marriage and the hope that the sins of the parents will not be visited upon the children.

Typical of the parents in all three plays are those in "The Sixth Year," for Lucy and Frank are parents of grown children. They are, at the moment, relatively prosperous, but their own relationship is, at best, unhealthy. Frank, a timid man, spent his life following his wife's orders; and, when he was unable to find a suitable job for himself, his wife got him one in her brother's business where he spent his career as a well-paid ornament. The result was a total loss of self-respect for Frank and frustration on Lucy's part because she had married a weak man:

LUCY: I'm sick and tired of your whining about how I destroyed your life for you! I made a man out of you! That's what I did!
FRANK: I don't think I'm very much of a man.
LUCY: I don't think so either. Let's just say I tried.[11]

When the play begins, Frank has just retired from his brother-in-law's business and has had time to think about his mistakes — and the love he has never received from his cold, domineering wife.

Lucy and Frank have a married daughter, Katherine Anne, who also faces a marital crisis. Her husband, Tom, has lost his job and has, as a result, gone into a severe depression. Tom is also from a prosperous family, and he cannot tolerate the fact that he has been unable to keep a job and must ask his wife to work so that they can maintain their apartment in a housing development. While Kathy works and tries to take care of the apartment and the children, Tom cannot face getting out of bed in the morning. After Tom disappears one night, Kathy takes the children to her parent's suburban home; and the rest of the play is a sad depiction of the failure of Kathy's parents' relationship when Kathy's problem brings theirs to a climax.

Lucy advises that Kathy take the reins as she herself had done many years ago:

You just be cold and hard. Because somebody has to be cold and hard. Somebody has to have a clear mind on what's to be done. Otherwise, there's just going to be yelling and recriminations and a lot of tears. . . . I'm afraid that's the way it's going to be for you the rest of your life. You might as well face that now.

KATHY: I don't think that's a very good basis for marriage.

LUCY: Your father and I have managed that way for thirty-two years with passing fair happiness. (II-20)

When Kathy's husband calls to tell Kathy that he has a night job in a factory, Lucy thinks Kathy should force him to take a job in the family business in Memphis; but Frank tells Kathy to go home and give her husband the love and support he needs: "I have lived a miserable, barren, loveless life. The endless bickering that I have indulged in makes me sick to my heart. . . . I never grew up to be a man. . . . I've been chasing this idea of being a man all my life, and now I know that there never was any such thing. If your mother had treated me like a man, I'd be a man. But your mother treated me like a dog, and that's what I am. That's why I want you to go to that boy. Don't make him come crawling to you like a dog" (III-6). The violent confrontation that occurs between her parents drives Kathy home to the arms of her husband and to a new beginning for a salvageable marriage.

There are many fine moments in "The Sixth Year," but the play does not ring true. All too often there are awkward pieces of self-analysis that sound more like Jules Feiffer's cartoons than serious drama — lines like "I feel we never had much of a father-daughter relationship" (I-18), or "Well, I'm not a bad looking guy, and we were attracted to each other. It was physical" (II-28) are sloppy exposition. We wonder, too, why the domineering mother had to come from the Tennessee Williams' South — especially when she was played by Sylvia Sidney. Chayefsky, in order to focus on the parents' relationship, presents too little about what Kathy and Tom are — why he failed in his jobs, or whether she will be able to be a supportive wife in a working-class existence that is alien to both of them. The play's strengths are the characterizations of the parents — the indomitable though unhappy mother and the father who knows himself all too well; but each one transcends the stereotype of the smothering mother and of the henpecked father. They are hampered, however, by a play that is not only haphazardly structured but sloppily written; for "The Sixth Year" did not receive the care Chayefsky usually lavished on his work.

Sylvia Sidney also played Grace Lipescu, the troubled stage mother in "Catch My Boy on Sunday." The younger, homelier, and ignored child in her own family, Grace has tried to compensate for her own feelings of inadequacy through the success of her husband and child. She had married her husband because he had outranked her sister's husband in the army, and now her only goal in life is making her twelve-year-old son a television star, not for his sake, but so she can have some sense of importance. At one point, Grace tells her sister about her husband: "He's a nice man, making the best of a bad bargain. I assure you he wishes he were out of it. Why should he love me? A nervous wreck of a woman, always in a bad temper. I don't even like myself, a woman with no beauty, brains or talent."[12] Her only sense of importance comes through her son's career, one she identifies with so closely as to confuse her pronouns in very revealing ways: "I got the part. They just called from N.B.C! I got the part!" (I-33).

Grace's misdirected ambition has driven a wedge into her marriage and is destroying her son who has become a serious behavior problem at school. Finally, Grace's husband asserts himself, puts a stop to Danny's career, and challenges Grace to master her own careers as wife and mother: "I love you, Grace, at least I did when we got married, so you must be pretty worthwhile on your own without having to use your son. On this basis, I think we can maybe work out a better relationship between us. I don't think you're an ugly duckling. I think you're a fine woman if you want to be" (III-16).

"Catch My Boy on Sunday" is more successful than its companion plays in this section because it is better focused: the play is Grace's, as it should be. All other characters are there only to deepen our understanding of her sense of inadequacy. Most of what we know about her son we discover through exposition, and her husband is presented only as he relates to her problem. Chayefsky has managed, too, to present Grace, not as the typical stage mother, but as a sympathetic woman driven by her own feelings of inferiority. She is not vicious, nor is she totally insensitive to those around her, but she is trapped in her own childhood. She is still trying to show her father that she deserves his love: "And if my father were alive today, and he could see Irene's children, and he could see my son Danny — well, I just wish he was alive today to see how wonderful I turned out with my children" (I-13). Typically, Grace's hope is through the love of her husband — through accepting his love, she might learn to love herself. "Catch My Boy on Sunday" may not have the vibrant quality of Chayefsky's best teleplays, but it is a well-crafted, convincing work about a situation that could have been mired in banal cliché.

The best known of these plays, in part because of its film incarnation with Bette Davis, is "The Catered Affair."[13] The basic situation of "The Catered Affair" is comic — the horrible result of a young couple's attempts to avoid a big church wedding — but the response of the parents to the situation gives the play a serious dimension. The setting is the Bronx, the home of Frank, a middle-aged cab driver, and his wife, Aggie. The marriage of Frank and Aggie was not a romantic attachment; rather it was arranged by Aggie's father with the help of a dowry of three hundred dollars, a fact Aggie has never let her husband forget. Frank is a kind man, but his relationship with his wife has never been a fulfilling one for her; and they had their familial and financial problems. One of their sons died in Korea; Frank's store went bankrupt; and he was forced to accept charity from Aggie's brother. Now Frank is terribly cautious about money, saving every extra penny to buy his own cab. There are still two children living at home, as well as Aggie's brother Jack, a middle-aged bachelor who boards with the family.

The delicate balance of family life is overturned when daughter Jane announces that she and her fiancé are going to be married in a few weeks so that they can take advantage of an opportunity to drive a friend's car to California. Jane and Ralph want a simple, quiet wedding; and Aggie is happy with their plan until subsequent events change her mind: Uncle Jack stalks out, furious at not being invited; the ladies at the market suggest that the quiet wedding is either the result of lack of necessary money or an indiscretion on the part of the young couple: "What is she getting married in the afternoon for? What's all the rush and all the secrecy?"[14] The last straw for Aggie comes when the groom's parents flaunt their generosity toward their children, for Aggie's pride and her guilt will not allow her to cheat her daughter out of something she feels the girl should have: "He's bought them an apartment and paid the year's rent, and he's making us look like pikers. And the truth is, Frank, what are we giving them, a check for some money? What have we ever given the girl?" (I-30). When Aggie decrees that there will be a big church wedding — whether the couple wants it or not — the problems begin.

The crises that ensue all have their roots in money. Aggie feels that no price is too dear for this last chance to show her love for her daughter, but Frank winces at every dollar to be spent from his cherished savings: "I have two thousand dollars for this wedding and not a penny more. I'm a hackie. I drive a taxicab. My wife may have given you the impression that I'm a direct scion of the DuPonts, but that's not true, really" (II-16). Jane's best friend cannot be in the wedding because it will cost too much money, and her fiancé is upset because the big wedding will destroy their plans for the trip to California. Finally, he presents the situation to Jane: "Now look, Janey. We're getting married, and this big wedding that your mother and father and my mother and father are cooking up has nothing to do with us. . . . Your mother is just feeling guilty about how she neglected you all your life, and she's just trying to buy a little love from you with this big spread . . . . I'll go along with this big wedding just so much. But when it means giving up our honeymoon, I think it's time to put an end to it" (II-27-8).

When Jane returns home, she delivers the verdict: "There's going to be no big wedding. Last night we decided to have a big wedding, and in one lousy day, my best friend hates me, my uncle won't talk to me, my mother and father are on the brink of annulment, I've lost my honeymoon, and my fiancé is so sore about the whole thing, I'll pretty well lose him" (II-33). Aggie's hurt at this decision is not easily assuaged for Frank's lack of support of her dream of a big wedding for her daughter has brought to the surface all her feelings of disillusionment and neglect by a husband who was given three hundred dollars to marry her.

Finally, Frank, who can sustain no more of his family problem, speaks frankly to Aggie: "I'm your husband. What about something to make me happy? You've been after that girl now for the last couple of years like it was the salvation of your soul. Well, she's going to be married, and the boy will be in the draft any day, and your brother Jack is moving out, and praise to his independence. And that's just me left for your old age. It's me you got to worry about" (III-14). When Sunday morning comes, the banns are to be announced, and the play ends with Aggie, dressed for church, watching her sleeping husband in their plain bedroom. No great resolution is presented, for Aggie will have to make the best of her lot.

There are some beautiful, touching moments in "The Catered Affair," but the effect is that of a pencil sketch of a complex painting. There are too many characters, too many emotions, for a short play. The result is that few scenes or characters seem developed, and the author has to settle too often for a pat explanation for motivation since there is no time for adequate development. The focal character is Aggie, who was beautifully played by Thelma Ritter; but she is not given time to develop. We are given no concept as to why this woman feels that she neglected her daughter beyond her statement that she has. Moreover, daughter Jane is far too vapid to be interesting; for, like Joe Manx's daughter in "The Big Deal," she is a stereotype of the healthy, loving daughter — far too healthy to be the product of parental neglect. If Chayefsky's major characters need more development, his less important personages offer some of the most touching moments when he demonstrates his ability to suggest an entire character in a few words and gestures: Jane's friend Alice tries to maintain her pride while she confesses that she cannot afford to be in the wedding; Uncle Jack decides that it is time he becomes independent; and the Hallorans brag about their generosity.

Since May, 1955, when "A Catered Affair" was aired, Chayefsky has been a rarity on television. His television adaptation of *Gideon* for "Hallmark Hall of Fame" in 1971 marked an all-too-brief return to the medium in which he had gained his early success. The withdrawal of such a talented writer was a great loss to the medium, for even his weakest plays offer examples of television's possibilities as a dramatic medium — as a vehicle for intimate domestic drama which, in a real sense, holds a mirror to the lives of its viewers. Moreover, the plays Chayefsky wrote for television in the mid-1950's represent the prevailing theatrical mode of the time, for the influence of Arthur Miller, Tennessee Williams, and the members of the Actors' Studio was at its strongest. While Chayefsky's teleplays are not in any sense equal to such fine stage plays as Williams' *Cat on a Hot Tin Roof* or Miller's *A View from the Bridge*, they offer small-scale examples of the sort of post-Freudian, domestic Realism that prevailed on Broadway. The best proof of Chayefsky's kinship to the legitimate playwrights is the success of his stage version of "Middle of the Night."

In the mid-1950's Chayefsky wrote, "It may seem foolish to say, but television, the scorned stepchild of drama, may well be the basic theater of our century" (132). Such a statement seems quixotic now, for television seems to have lost any former aspirations toward being a serious artistic medium. In doing so, it has surrendered the distinction that writers like Chayefsky gave it in its best years.

CHAPTER 3

The Dramatist of Disillusionment

THROUGH writers like Paddy Chayefsky, television drama achieved a great deal of respect in its early years. The plays also earned for their creators a celebrity far greater than that experienced by most writers for the stage or film. People looked forward to the next Paddy Chayefsky drama with an enthusiasm usually reserved for the appearance of a star. The result of this celebrity was the opportunity to write for the stage and the movies — the fruition of Chayefsky's early ambition. Chayefsky's route from television to film and to the legitimate stage was a new but not too unique phenomenon, since a Broadway hit during the late 1950's was often based on a television show. Such plays as William Gibson's *The Miracle Worker*, Gore Vidal's *Visit to a Small Planet*, and N. Richard Nash's *The Rainmaker* were expanded adaptations for the stage of earlier television plays. The plays had the virtue of audience familiarity — people were curious about seeing a live version of a show they had seen on television — and they offered their authors a valued opportunity to make their Broadway debuts as recognized quantities. In the late 1950's, the New York stage still had a prestige unequaled by any other performing medium; for, if a writer, no matter how successful elsewhere, wanted to be considered "serious," his work had to be tested on the legitimate stage.

When Chayefsky's *Middle of the Night* opened on Broadway in February, 1956, the writer had achieved celebrity not only on television but also in film; his adaptation of "Marty" had won the Academy Award for 1954. As he had done in his film debut, Chayefsky chose to begin his Broadway career with an adaptation of a television play. After the success of *Middle of the Night*, Chayefsky wrote only four more plays for the stage. The fifth, and in many ways the best, was never produced in New York.

Except for *Middle of the Night* and its successor, *The Tenth Man*,

Chayefsky's stage plays did not achieve great popular or critical success; and, after studying these plays, we surmise that the stage is not the most congenial vehicle for Chayefsky's vision. Chayefsky needs the close-up that focuses on a central character or on a meaningful detail, and he needs the freedom to work within a framework of short scenes. Through these techniques, he could focus effectively on the struggles of his central character. In the theater, Chayefsky always had difficulty balancing his desire to keep his central character in the foreground with his penchant for background detail.

In a sense, background is inessential to Chayefsky's plays; for they all are, in essence, attempts to depict one man's spiritual struggle. Whether the setting is Biblical Israel or revolutionary Russia, the basic conflict is the same — how does a man give his life meaning in a world that seems to rob him of any meaning? While this theme is hardly an original one, Chayefsky's plays are interesting, though imperfect, attempts to find the most effective dramatic form for his vision. Chayefsky wrote five extremely different plays: each presents a new perspective on what its creator sees as man's essential dilemma.

I Middle of the Night

A performance of *Middle of the Night* might look somewhat quaint today since the theater has eschewed the literal Realism that Chayefsky had espoused in his earlier career, and that television and the film had developed to its logical extreme. No great crises occur in the play, but the play's success is due in great part to its ability to involve us in the lives of its characters. The scope of the play is as limited as that of the lives of most of the audience; most of the conversation is empty, and most of the situations are even untheatrical. But there is a fascination in such a perfect reproduction of those sounds of urban life that indicate loneliness and frustration. Despite this photographic Realism, the basic action of *Middle of the Night* is extremely Romantic, a defiance of the world Chayefsky has created (or re-created) for his play.

Jerry Kingsley, the central character of *Middle of the Night*, seems from the outset to be almost painfully typical. He is a successful fifty-three-year old garment manufacturer. He is widowed; he has grown children, including a married daughter who is neurotically devoted to him; and he lives with his doting sister in a comfortable West Side apartment. Not surprisingly, Jerry Kingsley is an unhappy man who feels that there should have been and should be something more to his life than the sterile routine he has followed for decades. Moreover, he feels his manhood ebbing away: "I'll be sitting in a shop there, cutting a pattern, when suddenly, for no reason, I'll think, 'My God, I'm fifty-three years old. I'll be an old man with white hair soon. My life is coming to an end.' "[1] Visiting his family does not provide fulfillment, nor does the thought of marrying one of his sister's widowed friends "for companionship." Since he has watched his friends become obsessed about affirming their virility with young women, and since he has concluded that they have made fools of themselves in the process, Jerry fears being a foolish old man as much as he despises the emptiness of his present life.

An errand for the business takes Jerry to the apartment of one of the girls in the office, Betty Preiss, who is twenty-four years old, attractive, and married to a promising pianist; but, when we meet her, she, too, is unhappy. Betty has left her husband and returned to her mother's home because she has felt trapped in a marriage that is little more than a physical relationship. While her mother tells her, ". . . that's the whole thing, how you get along in bed" (7), Betty cannot be satisfied with what seems to her so little: "He doesn't know what to do with me, you know what I mean? There's no love or anything. Well, I can't stand that. I want him to love me. I want him to be pleased to see me. I want him to come home and tell me all that's happened to him and how he feels about things. And I want to tell him how I feel. I want something. I mean, is this what marriage is? Is this what life is? Boy, life isn't much if that's what it is" (39).

Part of Betty's frustration is due to the fact that George was the first man in her life. Because her father had left home when she was a small child, she thinks "I wanted poor George to make up for everything I never had in my life" (38). When Jerry goes to get some papers from Betty at her mother's apartment, Betty breaks down and tells him about her frustrations. Kingsley, out of sincere sympathy as well as a glimmer of attraction for the beautiful young girl, takes her out to dinner; and the inevitable situation develops with the inevitable problems. Jerry and Betty fall in love; and each expects from the other what each feels has been lacking in his or her life. Betty needs a father figure, and Jerry needs to feel loved by someone who can restore some vestiges of his male ego.

While a Freudian might consider their relationship a neurotic one, it is, for Chayefsky, better than the loneliness these people felt before they met. As for their families' reactions, Betty's mother is horrified at the thought of her daughter's dating a Jewish "sugar daddy"; and Jerry's family is outraged. Jerry's doting sister feels that her position is threatened; and his daughter's upset manifests itself in a quasi-Freudian analysis of her father's romance: "The relationship, to say the least, seems to be a neurotic one. The girl is obviously infantile in many ways. Otherwise she wouldn't have to look to older men. I don't know the girl, but obviously she is very dependent, very infantile. And the whole relationship doesn't sound to me like a sound marriage" (110). Finally, daughter Evelyn's harried husband explodes: "Boy, you're great! Sure, the trouble with Evelyn, she got a neurotic attachment! Holy Jesus Christ! He came to you, he says he's going to get married, and you whack him across the face with some two-bit psychology! . . . 'My father needs me!' You need your father, that's what!" (113).

While Jerry is fighting with his family, Betty is contending with her husband who only sees her defection as a threat to his manhood: "Your wife wants a divorce, the inference is that you failed her as a husband. That's a reflection on me as a man" (122). George attempts to get his wife to go to bed with him, thinking that a sexual rapprochement will solve everything; but Betty sees no possible reconciliation: "You need a girl who doesn't need you and I need too much from everybody. We're so wrong for each other, I wonder why we ever got married" (132).

All these family crises take place late in the night on which Jerry and Betty first make their relationship a physical one, an event that leads to additional complications since Jerry's fears of inadequacy make him impotent. Yet the love that Jerry offers Betty is far more important to her than the difference in their ages: ". . . maybe there's something wrong with loving an older man, but any love is better than none" (145). Despite all complications, Jerry and Betty decide to get married because "Even a few years of happiness you don't throw away" (145); and the play ends as their relationship begins.

In his review of *Middle of the Night*, Henry Hewes wrote:

In "Middle of the Night" Paddy Chayefsky has written less of a play than a
recognition of the whirlpools created within two ordinary human beings
when they suddenly realize that their urban existences are desperately
unsatisfactory. . . . Mr. Chayefsky doesn't find answers for everyone on
stage any more than everyone finds answers in life. . . . The playwright also
offers no formula for preventing the deterioration of love into the less
exciting man-wife relationship he finds to be the rule in society. And he
does not worry about Betty as a potential forty-year old widow. Rather, he is
content to use this romance as a foreground object against which to contrast
the more important background elements that make for crowded city loneliness.[2]

It is this contrast of Jerry and Betty's love with the loneliness of
those around them that makes Chayefsky's play so powerful. Despite the seemingly insurmountable problems facing Jerry and
Betty, their relationship is seen as being redemptive; for the world
around them is so empty, and its relationships so inadequate.
Betty's mother is depicted as a woman incapable of communicating
love to her children; her world is one of television, gossipy neigh-
bors, and her job at Hanscom's Bakery. When Betty asks for compassion, she gets self-pity and justification: "Your father abandoned me
with two little girls on my hands, one of them one year old. I had no
source of income. I have scrubbed floors for my two daughters. As
heaven is my witness, I have gone down on my knees and scrubbed
floors so my two children could eat" (8). For a woman who has
fought to survive, Betty's feeling of loneliness is incomprehensible
and unjustifiable; and Betty should "settle for" her life as others in
her circumstances have done. Her friend Marilyn offers the same
compromise: "You want to know what life is? You live, that's all.
That's life. You get married, you have kids — you get up in the
morning and you go to sleep at night" (65).
    Through such empty compromises, Chayefsky shows us the pain
of sensitive people who find the life they are offered inadequate for
their emotional needs. The repeated "What the Hell!" of Betty's
neighbor is more than an empty exclamation; it is a way of life that
Betty can't accept. Jerry may be more successful, but he knows that
a good job and an all-too-loving family cannot take the place of what
he needs: "I want to be loved by a woman, and that want dies hard.
When you give up that want, it's a very painful thing to go through"
(139). There is no eloquence in the dialogue of Middle of the Night,
no flights of imagery. The world Chayefsky gives us is mundane,

unpoetic; and the language reflects this world of things. Yet the dialogue effectively conveys the pain of the inhabitants of his sterile city.

Chayefsky was wise, too, in keeping his play within the claustrophobic confines of the principals' apartments. The walls that limit the action come to represent those that imprison the characters in a meaningless world. There is wisdom, too, in centering most of the action on one night and in alternating the simultaneous conflicts of Jerry and Betty within the same time period. The technique may be better suited to the electronic media, but here it creates the proper rhythm for a play that depends to a great extent on atmosphere.

The Broadway production of *Middle of the Night* benefited from the fine performance of Edward G. Robinson, but Joshua Logan's production often worked against the quiet tone of the play. Captions giving a scene's time and place were flashed on scrims, and a soap opera musical background cheapened the play. Despite the drawbacks of the production, *Middle of the Night* was a critical and financial success. The next challenge would be a move away from television material to an original stage play.

II The Tenth Man

The Tenth Man, Chayefsky's next and most successful play, opened in the fall of 1959; and it ran for a year and a half on Broadway despite some confusion with *The Best Man*, Gore Vidal's political melodrama which played in the theater across the street. There is a story, probably apochryphal about the man who turned to his wife halfway through Chayefsky's *The Tenth Man* and asked, "Which one is supposed to be Nixon?" For *The Tenth Man*, Chayefsky and the producers wisely engaged famed director Tyrone Guthrie to give the play the color and ritual it needed to be effective.

While *The Tenth Man* is not an adaptation, it is loosely based on that oft-revived classic of the Yiddish theater, S. Ansky's *The Dybbuk*. Ansky's play depicts the story of Leah, a young woman in an Eastern European Jewish community, who becomes possessed by the dybbuk (wandering spirit of a dead one) of Channon, the young man who loved her. In order to be joined with his loved one forever, Channon's spirit possesses Leah's body on the day of her wedding to another man. His spirit is exorcised in a theatrically effective cabalistic ritual; and, while Channon's spirit is forced from Leah, it is too strong to surrender her. He materializes before her, and Leah moves in her bridal gown toward the apparition and steps into the spirit world where she and Channon will be eternally one. Ironically, Leah is exorcised from bonds of the flesh rather than from the love of Channon's spirit.

In addition to the dramatic conflict, a philosophical conflict lies at the heart of the play. The dybbuk is not presented as an evil creature but as the embodiment of spiritual love. According to Channon — and to the playwright — "Everything created by God contains a spark of holiness."[3] There is good in all things, and the old Talmudic doctrine of good and evil creates a false antithesis. Channon's conquering of Leah's spirit through pure love also symbolizes victory over the good-evil doctrine of orthodox Judaism.

The success of *The Dybbuk* is based in great part on its highly effective combination of theatrical ritual and romanticism. The play uses a mythological evil spirit to negate evil and to affirm the power of love. Love is placed before God as the truly redemptive force. The message is brought to life not only through the characters but also through the effective use of the central myth and the exciting ritual of exorcism that is the play's climax. The play's continued popularity is also due to the finely etched portraits of the members of the Jewish community it depicts.

Chayefsky's *The Tenth Man* is also based on the possession of a young woman by a dybbuk, but here the conflict is between traditional faith and modern skepticism. As in *The Dybbuk*, the scene is a synagogue; but the synagogue is no longer the spiritual and cultural center of a community. It is in ill repair, and the rabbi must spend most of his time finding gimmicks to bring people to the temple: "I'm afraid there are times when I don't care if they believe in God as long as they come to the synagogue."[4] The Jews of Minneola, Long Island, clearly have lost the faith of their Old World forbears, for the only regular denizens of this temple are a group of old men who gather every morning for prayer. For the most part, these old men are immigrants from the old country who were reasonably successful and for whom religion is a ritual and a social event rather than a faith. One even claims to be an atheist as he prepares for services: "If I had something better to do, would I be here?" (9). Yet a couple of the men are quite devout, and all are knowledgeable about the lore of their religion. One of them, Hirschman, a cabalist, has spent most of his life in dedicated study of the mystic secrets of his religion. Clearly, whatever the attitudes of this group of men, they have close ties to the Old World of Ansky's play.

A rule in the Orthodox Jewish religion is that a *minyan*, a group of ten men, is necessary for a service. As the play opens, the old men are beginning their daily routine of looking for a few extra men so that they may begin their prayers. They are interrupted by the entrance of their crony, Foreman, who has brought his eighteen-year-old granddaughter. The granddaughter, Evelyn, is considered mad by her parents and her doctor, but Foreman is sure that she is possessed by a dybbuk. She claims to be Hannah Luchinsky, "the whore of Kiev," who has entered Evelyn's body because, "I want the strength of a pure soul so that I may acquire that experience to ascend to heaven" (22). Though some of the men think Evelyn is merely mad — "The last time I was up to Foreman's the girl confided to me in a whisper that she was Susan Hayward" (24) — the rest of them are excited about the possibility of an exorcism that would bring some interest into their lives.

As the men decide what to do, a young man, Arthur Landau, is brought by the sexton to be the tenth man at prayers. Arthur is in the throes of a nervous collapse; he has left his wife; he has tried suicide; he is now at the end of a three-day drinking bout; and all that sustains him now is faith in his analyst's ability to restore his equilibrium. Arthur, of course, sees Evelyn; discovers what the old men are planning to do; and strenuously objects to such a danger-ous, superstitious ritual. Arthur and Evelyn talk about each other's past and find themselves attracted to one another. Their God is Freud, and they discuss their psychopathological quirks with the same zeal that the old men bring to their religious disputations. Their language is a wry satire of armchair analysis, "I can hardly believe you are psychopathic? Are you very advanced?" (66)

Just as the old men believe a ritual will remove evil spirits, Arthur and Evelyn believe in their own ritual, but for them the white coat and analyst's couch replace the robes and the Torah. The only prob-lem is that the religion of the young couple doesn't seem to help them. They know the right words, but they are powerless to help themselves. As Arthur tells Evelyn, "Life is merely dreary if you're sane and unbearable if you're sensitive. I cannot think of a more meaningless sham than my own life" (69). Chayefsky has shrewdly

presented this scene in counterpoint to the prayer service which is
presented at the same time, and the litany of Freud is set against
that of Jahweh. Arthur leaves the synagogue after prayers, but he
has to return because "I just simply couldn't go till I knew you were
all right" (90). The lovers embrace while the cabalist chants in the
background: "For Thy salvation I hope, O Lord!" (90).

As the old men prepare for the exorcism, Arthur pits his modern,
rational materialism against their faith. After Arthur admits to believing in nothing, the cabalist tells him: "For you are a man possessed by the Tangible. If you cannot touch it with your fingers, it
simply does not exist. Indeed, that will be the epithet of your
generation — that you took everything for granted and believed in
nothing. It is a very little piece of life that we know. How shall I say
it? I suggest it is wiser to believe in dybbuks than in nothing at all."
But Arthur replies, "Mr. Hirschman, a good psychiatrist — even a
poor one — could strip your beliefs in ten minutes. . . . You have
invented it all — the guilt, God, forgiveness, the whole world, dybbuks, love, passion, fulfillment — the whole fantastic mess of pottage
because it is unbearable for you to bear the pain of insignificance"
(107).

The exorcism becomes, therefore, a battle between faith and rationality; but we know that Arthur's rationality has not enabled him
to survive intact in a world which renders man insignificant. As
Evelyn tells him, "You have some strange dybbuk all of your own,
some sad little turnkey, who drifts about inside of you, locking up all
the little doors, and saying, 'You are dead. You are dead'" (125).
For Chayefsky, Arthur's spiritual death is a result of his disbelief
in the one thing, love, that can give man significance; for Arthur
declares, "I love nothing!" (132). When the ten men are gath-
ered, the exorcism begins; and, in a colorful scene replete with
robes, black candles, and ram's horn, the cabalist banishes the evil
spirit.

The result, however, is somewhat surprising. Evelyn is unaf-
fected, but Arthur "begins to moan softly, and then with swift violence a horrible scream tears out of his throat. He staggers one brief
step forward. At the peak of his scream, he falls heavily down on the
floor of the synagogue in a complete faint" (150). By the traditional
religious rite that Arthur had scorned, he has been purged of the
spirits haunting him: "I feel as if I have been reduced to the moment
of birth, as if the universe has become one hunger" (152). Arthur,

left with the desire to live and with the will to love, will care for Evelyn: "Dybbuk, hear me. I will cherish this girl, and give her a home. I will tend to her needs and hold her in my arms when she screams out with your voice. Her soul is mine now — her soul, her charm, her beauty — even you, her insanity, are mine. If God will not exorcise you, dybbuk, I will" (153).

For Chayefsky, the dybbuk is not a vehicle for a religious theory; it is an image of anything that creates anguish within man. Arthur is as haunted as the schizophrenic girl who may or may not contain the spirit of Hannah Luchinsky. The exorcism, then, becomes a figurative purgation of those things that keep man from love. As the exorcism in Ansky's play made possible the union of the loving spirits, so in *The Tenth Man* does it allow Arthur and Evelyn to build a saving relationship.

The dybbuk is the structural principle of the play, and every character shows his outlook through his definition of this supernatural power. For most of the old men, it is a way to bring some excitement to their dull lives: it is an adventure as well as a link to the religion-centered life of the Chassidic community in which they grew up. For Foreman, the dybbuk is a means of explaining his granddaughter's madness — and a way of keeping her out of an institution: "Perhaps this produced a desperate susceptibility in me so that I clutch even at dybbuks rather than believe she is irretrievably insane" (32). The public relations-oriented rabbi would be happy to "believe once again in a God of dybbuks" (149). Arthur, of course, finds the dybbuk only a bizarre superstition, yet it is he who is freed of the spirits haunting him.

What gives *The Tenth Man* its tension is the fact that Chayefsky never lets his audience know whether the dybbuk does indeed possess Evelyn Foreman. While her mental history suggests that Hannah Luchinsky is merely another pathological aberration, the "whore of Kiev" sounds frighteningly convincing. Unless old Foreman regaled her with secrets of the youthful waywardness of some of his friends, Evelyn does indeed possess unique powers. Dybbuk or not, the exorcism does not work; it leaves love as the only remedy — with the help of psychiatry.

Certainly one of the interesting aspects of *The Tenth Man* is the change it manifests in Chayefsky's approach to the structure of his dramas. While he was extremely careful in his television plays to focus on one character and one situation, *The Tenth Man* is full of interesting characters. The play opens and closes with the old men, and it is they who dominate the play and maintain its underlying comic tone. Their alternation of religion with discussions of prospective grave-sites and with curses on their relations ("My daughter-in-law, may she grow rich and buy a hotel with a thousand rooms and be found dead in every one of them" [6]) provides a counterpoint to the anguish of Evelyn and Arthur. In fact, the tormented young couple seems far less important than the comic old men; and it is interest-ing to note that *The Tenth Man* was billed in New York as a comedy. Throughout, Chayefsky's gentle, humorous portrait of the old Jews seems to be his principal concern. Perhaps this emphasis is crucial to his presentation of his point of view toward the modern disaffec-tion he presents in Arthur Landau. The old men's lives may not be the most meaningful ones that the world offers, but their sense of tradition and perspective allows them to face life and death with equanimity. They may be comic, but they are not fools. Moreover, their old-fashioned exorcism proves to be far more successful than the younger generation's psychoanalysis.

The critical controversy that was waged over *The Tenth Man* centered on the play's shakiest aspect, Arthur's rather sudden and total conversion through love. While this transformation should be seen as part of a myth, just as the dybbuk is a myth, the Realistic trappings that are part of this modern re-telling of an old story tempt us to take the story literally. Robert Brustein wrote that the ending ". . . might have seemed less sentimental, flighty and evasive had the play remained within the confines of a fairy tale, but Chayefsky's object is to comment on the modern, particularly the Freudian, view of objective reality. Now Freud is open to criticism on many scores, but it can hardly be confuted by demonstrating that it is incompatible with a world which exists only in an author's fantasy."[5] The fact is that the play does not attempt to refute Freud, for even the old men are aware that, dybbuk or not, "The girl is a schizo-phrenic with violent tendencies" (6–7). Chayefsky's point is that Freud is no more or less valid than the cabalistic ritual, for man is supported by that in which he has faith. The only really critical state is one without faith — and without love.

Chayefsky has been criticized, too, for his presentation of love as the solution to all of man's problems regardless of kind or degree. Anatole Shub, in an article in *Commentary*, wrote: "Arthur with his education, his skepticism, his frustration with the whole range of secular values, signifies the rational person in a state of funk. Chayefsky, 'exorcising' him with a wave of the love-wand, seems to be saying to all people who have ever recognized a single intellectual or moral contradiction: 'See how simple it is? Why waste our time with your brains, when we common folk knew the secret all along.' "[6] Perhaps Arthur's speedy recovery from despair through his love of an eighteen-year-old schizophrenic who may also be possessed does seem too easy, especially since that recovery takes place through a ritual in which he has no faith.

If we look closely, however, the resolution of the play is quite meaningful; for Arthur's concern about and his strong sympathetic attachment for Evelyn make the exorcism a powerful experience for him. Evelyn, despite her psychic wounds, does have the two qualities Arthur needs — faith and love. While he is empty of any saving feelings or beliefs, Evelyn must be purged of her fantasies. Evelyn's love for Arthur gives him a reason to live; that change makes his response to Evelyn's exorcism a meaningful, positive one. Chayefsky works no miraculous cures in *The Tenth Man*, but he gives Arthur and Evelyn a reason to live and to fight their dybbuks. As old Alper says, "He still doesn't believe in God. He simply wants to love" (154). Arthur *wants* to love; that is the saving difference that Evelyn and the exorcism have made. It is this that links past and present, God and Freud — the need to be able to reach out to another human being. In Ansky's play, it is not the exorcism that triumphs but a love stronger than either man or evil spirits. Chayefsky has translated this concept to a more affluent but less happy society.

Chayefsky presents his concept and delineates his characters through his familiar ear for the dialogue of urban Jews. The rhythms and intonations are just right. Kenneth Tynan wrote that ". . . Mr. Chayefsky is a wonderfully creative listener. The best of his Jewish dialogue is as meaty as any I have heard since the heyday of Clifford Odets."[7] This sharpness of dialogue keeps the play from sinking into sentimentality. The language is always so apt and so strikingly familiar that we are drawn into a strong sympathy with the characters.

In Tyrone Guthrie's remarkably effective staging and with a superb cast comprised of some of the great veterans of the Yiddish theater and of some superb character actors, *The Tenth Man* ran well over a year and a half — an extremely healthy run for a straight play. Its success was based in part on its strong appeal to Jewish audiences, but also to its effectiveness on stage. The magazine *Time* called it "something not too frequent in the theatre: a genuine theatre piece."[8] Even the acerbic Gore Vidal, though he felt at odds with the theme, called its creator "a writer with a first rate imagination" and "a master of the theatre."[9]

The Tenth Man marked a turning point for Chayefsky: he had added a mythic dimension to his penchant for Realistic setting and dialogue. No longer satisfied with telling touching stories about average people, Chayefsky began to dig deeper, to try to lay bare the spiritual malaise that cripples many modern men. If his answers seem too pat for some, he had found a vivid means of presenting the questions dramatically.

III   Gideon

In 1961, Chayefsky tried to repeat the success of *The Tenth Man* with another treatment of the Jewish people's relationship to their faith; and he chose as his starting point the familiar Old Testament story of Gideon. The Book of Judges tells us that Gideon was chosen by Jehovah to save His people from the Midianites. Gideon was "the least in [his] father's family,"[10] but Jehovah wanted a miracle to occur through the agency of an ordinary man so that the Hebrews would marvel at His miraculous work. Gideon did his Lord's bidding and saved the people of Israel from the Midianites. After his triumph, he made a golden ephod (vestment) for the Lord and enshrined it. Ignorant and ungrateful, the Israelites worshipped the ephod as a graven image and soon forgot "the Lord their God who had delivered them from enemies on every side."[11] Chayefsky has taken this simple story and transformed it into a highly theatrical debate between the Old Testament Jahveh and a simple, ordinary man who cannot surrender his pride. Gideon is certainly the least in his father's family, for he is a plodding, doltish, but good-humored man. He enters just as his people are crying to God for a savior to protect them from an imminent Midianite invasion. God, we find, has chosen this bumbling man to be the savior of His people and sends His message to Gideon through His angel. Gideon is not quick to believe in this angel, nor is he impressed with the God it represents: "A farmer, you see, needs a romping god. And Yahweh, as I recall, was grim"[12]. God tells Gideon that He has decided to give His wayward, idolatrous people another chance to live His way; and, when the Midianites approach, Gideon stands before his ter- rified people as their new savior.

The miracle God asks Gideon to oversee is somewhat bizarre — three hundred men with lamps and trumpets are to confront the Midianite army of thousands. God wants not only a victory, but a miracle: "It shall not be said, when this victory over Midian is won, that it was won by Gideon or any other general. This victory shall be mine. It shall be a miracle. It shall be clear to all Israel that only the hand of God delivered them" (39). The Midianites are devastated, and Gideon is made the hero of his people, a position he naturally enjoys but one which leads him into conflict with God. This victory is to be God's alone, but Gideon finds such humility increasingly difficult: "There is no honor that reflects to me in it at all, merely that I am beloved of God" (71). Gideon wants a sense of personal significance that God will not grant him: "Do not presume to mat- ter, Gideon, for in the house of God you matter not. . . . To love me, Gideon, you must abandon all your vanities. They are presumptu- ous and will come between us" (71–72).

The Israelites' conflict with the Midianites is replaced by man's conflict with Jehovah as Gideon finds Jehovah's orders more and more demeaning. Conflict becomes impasse when Gideon cannot bring himself to kill the traitorous elders of Succoth as God has ordered: "I cannot do it. Let them live, Shellem, scourge them, if you will, with whips, with briars of the wilderness and thorns. For surely man must have more meaning than this" (113). Gideon re- turns home to his family, frustrated by the need to give God the credit for the victories. He tells the angel that he must reject his love for God: "I cannot love you, God, for it makes me a meaning- less thing" (128). With this renunciation, Gideon loses his ability to see the angel; and his last entreaty to the God he can no longer see is: "If you love me, let me believe at least in mine own self!" (136). When Gideon goes away with his family, putting on the ephod he made for God, the Angel is left alone on stage to present God's necessary acceptance of man's willfullness: "God no more believes it odd / That man cannot believe in God. / Man believes the best he can, / Which means, it seems, belief in man" (137–38).

While *Gideon* is a play of mixed blessings, it does present another dimension of Chayefsky's exploration of the anatomy of faith. In *The Tenth Man*, Chayefsky gives us an essentially godless world; for

even the Orthodox old men are skeptical about the religion they
practice. The play's resolution, placed within a religious context, is a
secular one since the saving emotion is love for another human
being and since this love is equated with belief in God: "When you
stop to think about it, gentlemen, is there any difference?" (154).
Gideon, however, is about a man's relationship with a very real
God. If anything, Chayefsky dramatizes through the play why man's
estrangement from God is an inevitable part of human history: God
created man with a free will, but human freedom and obedience to
God are antithetical. In *Gideon*, we also find a new dimension that
will dominate Chayefsky's later plays: a basic impulse in *Gideon* is
man's desire to give his life some meaning, some significance; therefore, Gideon must reject a God who sees man as nothing more than
His pawn.

In an interview at the time of *Gideon*'s opening on Broadway,
Chayefsky said, "My play is not about God testing Gideon. It's
about Gideon testing God."[13] The comment was pertinent since
Gideon was often compared to Archibald MacLeish's recent success,
J.B., an adaptation of the Book of Job. MacLeish's play makes the
Biblical Job a successful American businessman who is cruelly
tested by God to prove his faith. Unlike the Biblical Job, who keeps
his faith despite God's vicious whimsy, MacLeish's hero renounces
both the submission and the blind acceptance that God demands
and the cynical defiance epitomized by Satan. At the end, J.B.
realizes that life is a mystery not easily explained by God and that
human love is man's only support. God in *J.B.* is the voice in the
whirlwind shouting down J.B.'s demand for a reason for his suffering.

Chayefsky's God does not cruelly test his hero, as does Mac-
Leish's, but He makes demands that are impossible for His creatures to fulfill. Chayefsky's God wants love and total submission,
and the love He demands is more than reverence: "I demand a
splendid love from you, abandoned adoration, a torrent, a stream of
love" (54). This demand for total devotion from man allows man no
reason for his existence beyond pleasing God: "Know that there is a
God, and that His will is all there is" (130). The history of the
sufferings of the Hebrew people is attributable to God's punishment
for man's failure to love Him totally. Chayefsky's point is that this
God asks too much of man: ". . . it is not an easy thing to love God,"
Gideon says. "One must transcend all the frailties of man" (108).

Gideon's apostasy would not be so sympathetic were it not for the fact that he realizes that this Jahweh robs man of meaning by allowing man meaning only through Him. When God demands to know why Gideon defied His order to kill the elders of Succoth, Gideon presents a moving argument for his need to separate himself from God: "I raised my spear above their heads, but in that moment I felt a shaft of terror that chills me even now. It was as if the nakedness of all things were exposed to me, and I saw myself and all men for what we truly are, suspensions of matter, flailing about for footholds in the void, all the while slipping back screaming into endless suffocations. That is the truth of things, I know, but I cannot call it truth. It is too hideous, an intolerable state of affairs" (127–28).

God demands a love from man that robs man of essential aspects of his personality, including a sense of importance and a reason for living. Living at God's whim is not different enough from being overcome by meaninglessness. What is interesting here is that Gideon does not question whether God is right. He will accept his illusion of importance in the face of God's truth and in defiance of God's wrath which he knows is quite real, for he has been an instrument of that wrath. Faced with the loss of a sense of meaning, man will defy God Himself. It is at this moment that Gideon is a courageous hero rather than at his moment of glory against the Midianites. It is at this point, too, that Gideon tests God. Can God truly love His creatures and lovingly grant them a sense of importance, however imaginary that importance is? Can God love as a father rather than as a domineering mother or a jealous wife? It is interesting to note that God refers to Himself in feminine terms: "Consider how you have already reduced me to some kind of clever if wanton lady who finds you handsome and sends you into battle with her handkerchief" (72). God tells Gideon, "I love all men. It is my essence" (66), but that love does not allow man any essence. However, at the end, God allows Gideon his freedom and his illusion of importance without withholding His love.

Chayefsky's challenge was to make this somewhat churlish God into a valid theatrical presence. To this end, he personified God through a black-robed angel who serves as God's earthly "personation." Through this reduction, we see God's love, His wrath, and His demands in human terms. This presentation may be seen as theologically unsound, but Chayefsky's conflict between Gideon and God is built on the premise that man can only see God on very human terms. God was rejected by Gideon's ancestors in favor of idols because idols were tangible and easier to grasp than an invisible, abstract, demanding Jehovah. Gideon can love God, but only in human terms, as a man loves a lover; he cannot return divine love. In a sense, Chayefsky's device of the angel allows us to see God through Gideon's eyes and to share with him the vision he alone had.

Perhaps equally as difficult as creating a credible deity was the task of giving Him a human adversary who was both ordinary and sympathetic. Gideon begins as a bumbler, but he is never a fool. His frailties make us realize the enormity of God's miraculous engineering of the victory over the Midianites, but his discomfort with God's demands engages our sympathy. When the angel first confronts Gideon, Gideon says: "I have never asked of any god more than my own, that my trees bear olives, that my ewes bear lambs, the natural increase of things, no special favor" (20). Gideon is not a spiritual man; he wants a god that will support his material needs; but through his conflict with God, he realizes that he has greater needs: "I must aspire, God" (135). His aspirations are not great; he wants the love of those around him and a sense of a place in a rational world. For these, he will defy God Himself.

In *Gideon*, Chayefsky has managed to tell his story with characteristic economy. While the play has a large supporting cast, the focus is kept on the two adversaries. The dialogue is quite different from the contemporary urban idiom identified with Chayefsky. In writing the play, Chayefsky labored over the language: "The first time I wrote it I tried to keep the authentic archaic dialogue, but it was quite portentous. . . . It was terribly difficult to make it colloquial and yet keep it away from the modern idiom."[14] This difficult balance is maintained admirably in Gideon's dialogue. Prosaic, yet often eloquent, the dialogue characterizes Gideon as a simple man; but his speech has a timeless quality that is achieved in part by balancing a simple sentence structure with a varied, often complex vocabulary: "And he told me some wild farrago of things concerning the temporal inadequacies of man, now, was and is and all manner of things like that" (108). God, of course, is given elevated language, one often directly from Judges. There are times when He is given language that is truly poetic, such as the long speech beginning, "Gideon, I pray you, do not scorn me!" (134).

Gideon was not a success in New York, but it had a respectable two-hundred–performance run. Many critics disapproved of Chayefsky's reduction of a Great Debate to one between a nagging God and a middle-class American Gideon. Robert Brustein in a scathing review attacked the play as crass catering to mass taste: "It would not surprise me if Chayefsky, before writing *Gideon*, had made a sociological depth study of upward cultural mobility among the newly rich, the growing religiosity in the suburbs, and just how much rebellion an audience is willing to tolerate before running for the exits. In his new play he has managed to unify all three columns of the questionnaire (*Yes, No,* and *Undecided*) by combining secular sentiments with religous pieties, vaudeville effects with Herman Wouk metaphysics, and the titillation of revolt with the security of conformity."[15]

While amusing, Brustein's review attacks the play for having its roots in the American Realistic theater rather than in European closet drama. Chayefsky's point is that the struggles of ordinary men are valid topics for drama, and Gideon did not have to be a titan because he is an historical figure. Moreover, since our era has little belief in heroic rebels, Chayefsky has given us a view of God that has a validity for many modern men, a hero who is typical of much of his audience, and a play about their conflict that is an effective theatrical experience. As the reviewer for *Theatre Arts* wrote, "He [Chayefsky] has turned a skimpy story, easily read in a few minutes, into a full, exciting evening in the theatre by breathing a remarkable degree of life into his two protagonists. They are what matters and they matter terribly."[16] What may matter is that Gideon leaves the stage knowing that to live meaningfully and happily he must believe in the illusion that his life has some significance, that he has some control over his destiny. These illusions Chayefsky investigates through another historical character in his next play.

IV   The Passion of Josef D.

"We Socialists, it would seem, have only proclaimed another religion, and, like other religions, ours is just a contrivance to satisfy our presumption to be meaningful."[17] As this statement indicates, the core of Chayefsky's *The Passion of Josef D.* is the question that dominated *The Tenth Man* and *Gideon:* how does man live with any sense of meaning? In *The Tenth Man*, man had to love, to reach out to another person to fill a void that neither traditional religion nor contemporary psychoanalysis could fill. *Gideon* showed man as defying even his God to find meaning through the illusion of control and understanding of his destiny. *The Passion of Josef D.* eliminates the possibility of belief in God, but it demonstrates that some men create their own gods to fill the void; for this play shows a social upheaval that sprang, not from a miracle of Jahveh, but from human appetite. In the process of dealing with these rather large issues, *The Passion of Josef D.* presents a rather troubling picture of the chaos of human history and the forces that shape it.

The Passion of Josef D. alternates scenes depicting crucial moments in the life of Josef Stalin with quasi-vaudeville numbers that give a humorous perspective on the Russian Revolution. While the dramatic scenes present a compelling, insightful picture of the forces at work within the central character, the vaudeville routines present Chayefsky's version of the essential absurdity of such a revolution as the one that Stalin helped create. This sense of absurdity is heightened by the circular structure of the play; for it opens with the Russian people's singing a litany-like prayer to Tsar Nikolai, and it ends with Stalin leading the people in the same litany, now addressed to Lenin.

The play opens with a brief introductory scene in which Nadya Alliluyeva leads a confrontation with a battery of the Tsar's soldiers. The crowd of people with Nadya begin to change from being docile, long-suffering Russian peasants to revolutionaries:

> The pious Russian brute now slowly stirs.
> Enough's enough for even Russian clods.
> O Christ! O Tsar! O Russian Lords and Sirs!
> The devil take you all! We'll have to manage without gods.
>
> (9)

This rather cynical stanza is crucial for setting the revolution in the perspective in which Chayefsky wants us to see it. The Russian Revolution is predicated not only on hunger; but on a loss of faith that makes the suffering intolerable. If one god won't help, the people will turn to another; and, as we shall see, the religious dimension of the revolution is the most dangerous.

We meet Stalin on March 22, 1917, the day of his release from the Siberian shack in which he has been held a political prisoner. We discover through his discussion with the constable that the squalor of his childhood, not intellectual theories, have made him a revolutionary: "We paid one ruble a month for our hut. That was all that divided us from the dogs that evacuated outside our door; they didn't pay rent. I don't have to cultivate my class hatred, by God. I came by it in the blood" (15). After discussing his past with the constable, Stalin knifes him in the back for his boots, a grotesque act that not only shows us Stalin's amorality but also comments on the essence of revolution: "When a barefoot fellow tells you he is revolting against tyranny, watch out: he's only after your boots" (17). After a weak musical number that depicts the factionalism of Russian Socialists, Stalin is reunited with Nadya, who is eighteen and who is a devout revolutionary, as well as the daughter of revolutionary allies. The revolution to her is devout doctrine which she recites like a catechism, but Marxist doctrine is not enough for her; Nadya's real love, that for which she will sacrifice everything, is not a theory but her love for Josef Stalin, which as we see from its beginnings, is doomed. While Nadya talks of glorious Lenin and the salvation of Russia, Stalin rips off her blouse and makes a brutal pass at her.

The Stalin we see in these early scenes is a nihilistically cynical man. Totally without illusions, he regards the revolution as a way of life: "In my time, a boy either cobbled or carpentered or apprenticed out to a terrorist society. We have hundreds of them" (38). Unlike the zealous believers like Nadya or the factionalist hairsplitters, Stalin is without ideals or theory: "Well, the fact is I'm just a party tough" (38). What we discover, however, is that Nihilism is intolerable for a man who needs a god. When Stalin tells Nadya of the anguish of his reaction toward his wife's death, he tells us of the void that must be filled: "My wife died. I was plunged into terror. Beyond despair. A man can endure life if there is a reason for it, even an incomprehensible one. But to suffer for no reason at all is too hideous. . . . I could not endure to live without a god" (64). The god comes in the form of Lenin, a sensitive intellectual who has learned to live without a god, but who chooses another saving illusion, that of man's goodness and man's control of his destiny. In their first confrontation Chayefsky deftly presents the conflict between the man who must have a deity and the one who is a true humanist. When Stalin tells Lenin of his expulsion from a seminary,

Lenin comments: "The renegade priest is often the most fanatic.
Having abandoned one god, he is all the more famished for the next.
. . . We Bolsheviks do not require gods to explain the brutalities of
men. Men manufacture their own sufferings; men can correct them"
(74). Despite his fear of men like Stalin, Lenin knows that the
revolutionary fanatic must supplant the intellectual theorist if social
change is to be effected.

Despite Lenin's protestations, Stalin finds his new god in the
charismatic intellectual, a god that supplants even his feelings for
Nadya: "You're a smashing girl, Nadinka. But the best I could get
out of you would be pleasure. Lenin makes me meaningful, not so
transient a satisfaction. He has this gift, eh, to make one feel significant. That's all any man needs a god for, I think" (85–86).

When the third act takes place, five years after the revolution,
Lenin is a sick man, the victim of two strokes; and Stalin has begun
his reign of terror to pave the way for his takeover as Lenin's successor. His power is kept by violence; and the greatest victim of it is his
wife, Nadya, who is driven nearly insane by Stalin's cruelty and
neglect. The scene is one of disillusionment over the past and of fear
for the future because Lenin, aware of the failure of his revolution to
change the lot of the people, has realized that humanism is as foolish
as any other religion. To Lenin, humanism is only another illusion
that gives man's life a meaning: "Our Russian revolution was a revolution of humbugs. Lord, why do we insist on being meaningful
creatures? Since there is no truth we know that bears that out, we
assume there must be a truth we don't know that is more accom-
modating. That, I think, states the case for God. But you and I,
Nadya, were even more corrupt than that. We know there is no
God, so we reasoned ourselves to be ultimate. That, I think, states
the case for humanitarianism. We looked back over our thousand
years of impotent constancy, and nevertheless insisted we'd been
improving all the while" (97).

Lenin is strong enough to settle for the essential meaninglessness
of life, but those around him are not. Nadya, despite all her disillusionment, must love Stalin; for that gives her something, however
meager, to live for: "You're a poet, Vladimir Ilyich. To you terror is
passionate and credible. But for those of us not poets, life is too
transient to be believed. It requires extraordinary faith — more,
anyway, than I have. My love for Stalin, you see, is the only act of

faith I'm capable of" (100). Nadya wants Stalin's power taken away because she cannot live without his love which has been supplanted by his worship of Lenin; but Lenin wants Stalin robbed of power because of the cruelty of his religious fanaticism: "You must do without gods and truth, Stalin! You must give them up! If there is a god, he'll have to manage for himself! We've got our own imperfect, impermanent and thoroughly unsatisfactory world to deal with!" (107–08). Lenin, however, dies before Stalin can be crushed; and the disciple assumes the role of dictator. He intends to govern by making Lenin a god for all and by keeping himself as his god's earthly representative. The play ends with a litany to Lenin, a strange reversal of the opening chorus to the Tsar.

As this synopsis suggests, *The Passion of Josef D.* is an extremely ambitious play, perhaps too much so. Chayefsky's preliminary notes for the work comprise a lengthy history (over five hundred typed pages) of the gestation of this large-scale work. The notes show, too, how Chayefsky conceived his work after he had had the idea of a play about Lenin and had obviously researched extensively into the Russian Revolution and its principal architects. At the outset, the play was to chronicle Lenin's rise to power and his realization that his goal of improving mankind was merely an illusion: "So in the end, Lenin knows his dream of achieving Paradise on earth is all a fraud and an illusion."[18] With this focus came the controlling idea for the play: "in other words, the play is a plea for reality — It says our science and our knowledge are splendid devices, not absolute truths. The play's plea, then, is why must we have absolute truths? — Let God have absolute truths — As men, we must function within probabilities and uncertain truths. . . ."[19] As Chayefsky's concept of Lenin developed, the one about Stalin grew as well: "Stalin is Stalin, a brute and we must let him be that way — It was making him think he could be a noble creature that caused all the trouble. . . ."[20]

After days and pages and pages of notes, Chayefsky changed the focus of his play: "Let's face it — It is Stalin's show — ."[21] The next four hundred pages of notes shape the play around this brute whose Christianity shaped his need for a god and whose willingness to sacrifice all to his illusion gave him meaning. Chayefsky did not merely want to write a play about one man, however; he wanted to write about the Russian Revolution as the bloody price men pay for their illusions and their sense of moral superiority. And this second desire dictated the structure of the play, a structure that owes much to the epic theater of Berthold Brecht.

Brecht's "epic theater" has become so much a part of our modern theatrical language that we sometimes forget its origins. Influenced greatly by the director, Erwin Piscator, Brecht wanted to create a theater in which the audience surrendered its desire to escape through theater in favor of an experience which the audience would analyze and judge. The play was to be the demonstration of social phenomena that could be changed, and an objective never to be forgotten was that the theatrical experience was merely a simulation of an experience, not an experience. This awareness would be maintained through the use of all the tricks of the theater — film, cabaret acts, elaborate stage machinery, titles projected on overhead screens, narration, and projected cartoons — and linear plot development was sacrificed for a succession of tableaux. The principal desire was to challenge the audience's intellect rather than to move it to pity or to fear.

The epic theater was a perfect form for Brecht who was far more interested in complex patterns of action that reflect basic social phenomena than in delineating individual characters; but his great plays, like *Mother Courage*, do that as well. Chayefsky's strength is character portrayal that engages the audience's interest and sympathy, the very effects that Brecht tried to counter with his theory of alienation. Moreover, Chayefsky's roots are in American Naturalism, not German Expressionism. As a result of Chayefsky's capabilities and interests, the successful moments in *The Passion of Josef D.* are those which dispense with theatrical tricks and present absorbing portrayals of two fascinating historical figures.

In Shavian fashion, Chayefsky makes his characters mouthpieces for his own vision of history; but he is, in his strongest scenes, able to hold us with the force of his ideas despite his divergence from historical fact. The third act, with its confrontations between Lenin and Nadya, and then between Lenin and Stalin, is absorbing theater. Chayefsky is most successful in small-scale confrontations, and these count among his best scenes for the stage. Moreover, in these scenes Chayefsky has taken another approach toward his dialogue; he has removed himself altogether from the American colloquial and has replaced it with a somewhat mannered but vivid language. The vocabulary is massive and ornate, and Chayefsky is not averse to having the peasant Stalin say, "What a baroque demonstration," if it strikes his fancy. Chayefsky has also characterized Stalin's speech by using a few simple idiosyncrasies like the constant "eh?" at the end of the sentence or by employing short sentences and colorful imagery, as in this sentence: "In the end it always turns out you were a sensible old peasant who knew where the crayfish hid in the winter" (71). Except for Stalin's worship of Lenin, his language characterizes him as being earthy and curiously devoid of emotion.

In his preliminary notes for *The Passion of Josef D.*, Chayefsky makes some comments about the Russian language that are particularly pertinent to his treatment of Stalin: "The one thing one must remember about Russians is that they never feel they have quite made their point — so they add adjectives for further clarity, then superlative endings for emphasis and then exclamation points, because, by now, the adjectives and superlative endings have diffused the original point."[22] Lenin's language characterizes him as a passionate man with his rhetorical questions, his repetition of key words, his constant mandates loaded with exclamation marks: "Yes! It can be done. Peace! Land! All power to the Soviets! This is the tide of affairs!" (73). Even his disillusionment is rhetorical: "Self-preservation is the principle of life. We have only to aspire to that and it will be the saving of all of us. We are knowledgeable creatures. We are capable of self-preservation" (108).

Despite the grand scale of *The Passion of Josef D.*, there are only two major roles. Nadya serves only as a foil for Stalin, the man who would renounce even love for a false god. Most of the other characters are part of the less successful dimension of the play — they appear in the pseudo-Brechtian music hall turns. In one, Trotsky is presented as a ham actor who takes all credit for a production called "the revolution": "I not only played the leading role, I also costumed and choreographed the entire revolution, simply staged every minute of it really" (77). In a play that so successfully brings Stalin and Lenin to life, it seems a bit odd to reduce Trotsky to a cartoon figure. Such a depiction not only puts the historicity of the entire play into doubt but removes Trotsky from his rightful dramatic place as a foil to Lenin and Stalin — as the unrealistic idealist whom both Lenin and Stalin mistrusted. Another musical number, "Nothing Has Changed," has a Russian capitalist slash his wrists, blow his brains out, and hang himself as a symbol of the suicidal affiliation of the bourgeoisie with the Socialists. The scene belabors a rather obvious point, but the real problem is that it has nothing at all to do with the essential conflict of the play. There is no reason for the audience to care about the fate of the Russian businessman; it is interested in Stalin and needs only such background as is needed to support Chayefsky's interesting picture of this fascinating man.

Indeed, Chayefsky's alternating historical satires merely intrude. Chayefsky was trying to place Stalin in an historical context by using Brechtian methods, but Chayefsky's play is not really about how external events affected his central character; it is about how Stalin's particular psychological makeup and spiritual malaise motivated him to affect external events. The play is about a man who takes the easy way out of a spiritual crisis, who chooses idolatry rather than responsibility. As Nadya tells Lenin, "It's easiest of all to believe in gods, eh? That requires no faith at all" (101). Such a subject is best served by an unwavering focus on the central character rather than by an extravaganza.

There are times, too, when Chayefsky seems to find the easy solution to end a scene. He tends to end important scenes with asides to the audience which give the "moral" of a scene. These both cheapen the scene and insult the intelligence of his audience. If a scene doesn't make its own point, it is a failure and cannot be improved or justified by tacking on an explanatory epigram. Indeed, *The Passion of Josef D.* was a failure with most critics and at the box office. The play suffered from some major miscalculations, but it presents not only a fascinating picture of yet another man in search of definition but also, within its gaudy framework, some of Chayefsky's best scenes. As Henry Hewes has observed, what can be appreciated are ". . . the scope of the material, the fresh insight, the performances, and here and there stretches of the sort of superior dialogue that has made Mr. Chayefsky one of our best playwrights."[23] Chayefsky later wrote that "It is entirely possible that man will destroy himself in order to preserve his own dignity. That was what my play was about."[24] It is very difficult, if not impossible, to write a play about man rather than a man. If Chayefsky had kept the spotlight on his central characters and had let the audience do the generalizing, he would have given us that brilliant play of which we see glimmers in *The Passion of Josef D.*

V   The Latent Heterosexual

The Passion of Josef D. offered man only the bleak possibilities of facing the terror at the heart of existence in a godless world or of choosing an illusion to give his life some justification. Unfortunately, such illusion and justification can be quite dangerous; for Stalin chose to make a god out of Lenin to justify his own life and the cruelty necessary to maintain his illusion. Nowadays, few charismatic figures exist or appear, and man is more likely to worship mammon than Lenin. This worship of a capitalistic god Chayefsky chose to treat in his next play, *The Latent Heterosexual*, in which John Morley, the central character, is a magnificent if bizarre nonconformist. He is a large man on whom blatant effeminacy becomes grotesque caricature. After years of meditating in Egyptian deserts, of waiting tables in Marakeesh, and of trying to write the Great Work, Morley has become successful. His latest book — a statement of man's search for serenity that is achieved, it seems, primarily through fellatio and sodomy — has become a best seller. The book is entitled *A Corporation of Cadis*, a strangely ironic combination of materialism and romanticism and an augury of things to come; for Morley's royalties have bought a large house on the Hudson River which he and his roommate have converted into a seralgio-like edifice in which they can indulge their propensity for near-Eastern theatrics and narcotics. The rest of the money has been converted into various types of gold coins from which Morley achieves an almost sexual pleasure. Unfortunately, none of Morley's new-found wealth has found its way into the hands of the Internal Revenue Service, a fact that august body has recently discovered; and the miserly Morley wants to avoid losing any of his precious fortune.

Morley's dilemma thrusts him into an alien but, for him, an extremely attractive world — the world of accountants and tax lawyers. These men provide Morley with the solution to all his problems with the government by turning him into a corporation full of loopholes and tax dodges. Not only does this corporate identity offer Morley some refuge from the ravages of taxation; he regards it as the peace of mind he has for so long sought, a spiritual transcendence like that he sought years before in the desert: "I've spent my life trying to retrieve that serenity in the desert. Not until now have I felt so transfigured!"[25] But one peculiar aspect of Morley's corporate identity is that it requires a marriage for the sake of joint returns rather than for his personal comfort.

The future bride is Christine Van Dam, a highly successful "call girl" whose phenomenal success in her chosen profession has forced her to incorporate and to marry. While Morley does not care for a shady lady whose traipsing around his home would scare his room-mate, he will accept this discomfort for the sake of the corporate identity: "My God, you boys are on to something ultimate here, don't you know it? I tell you, I felt it the first moment I came in here — a sensation of beatitude, of illuminated innocence. One avoids nervous breakdowns because they are not deductible; one writes books because they are; one marries for the joint tax declaration; one divorces for the property settlement. My God! Don't you realize the apocalyptic clarity of all that?" (29–30).

Morley recognizes that the ultra-materialism of the lawyers and the accountants is the modern religion complete with "Ten Commandments" furnished by the Internal Revenue Service and that this new religion gives a lost modern man a way of life. However, like the dictates of Gideon's Jahweh, the strictures of a corporate identity rob a man of all the characteristics that comprise his individuality. At first, Morley sees his transformation as something beautiful: ". . . I've just felt the strangest mythopoeic feeling. Do you know how, in Greek myth, heroes are forever being turned into trees and nymphs into waterfalls? Well, I swear to you, Arthur, I have the feeling as I sit here that some sort of physical reconstruction is going on in me" (60). Slowly, however, the transformation, becomes more like a Kafka novel than a Greek myth; for John Morley, who came into the accountant's office an eccentric, slowly becomes a depersonalized cog in the corporate machine. His marriage to Christine brings about a conversion from an effeminate homosexual to a cigar-smoking ultra-masculine character in a lumber jacket. Heterosexual relationships have made John an epitome of manliness, but his relationship with Christine results in a stillborn child — a fitting, almost symbolic, issue of a marriage made by an accountant. The shock of the stillborn child not only speeds John's transformation but also separates him from the rest of humanity.

As his troubled wife tells his accountant, "Well, he stopped being a faggot, he kicked the junk, and he hasn't written a word since last spring. He's the husband of a whore, the father of a dead son. I mean, the only thing that's real to him any more is this corporation of his. He talks about it like it was alive" (66). Morley has moved out of his home into his office, and his priestly garb is a three-piece dark suit. All has been sacrificed to his new identity: ". . . I'm withdrawing into the sanctity of my corporate identity which I find superior to my human identity" (75). The result is little more than John the machine who jerkily signs documents and who now relates to nothing but the litany of corporate jargon. Eventually, for the corporation, he divorces Christine; but by this time he can communicate with no one. His catatonia is broken only by news of the corporation, but the stupor brings him not peace but unrelieved anguish: "If I had to describe Mr. Morley's condition, I would say he lives constantly exposed to the ultimate terror of life which is the existential state of all men. It must be insufferable" (113). Even suicide is impossible, for Morley can initiate nothing; and only one way exists to bring Morley to put an end to his suffering: the high priest of the corporation, the tax accountant, has but to say the right incantation: "It would be of great benefit to your corporation if you were to die" (114). The right words spoken, Morley is empowered to commit a priestly ritual suicide — hara-kiri with a pair of garden shears.

The Latent Heterosexual presents a rather grim vision; for, like Arthur Landau in *The Tenth Man* and Josef Stalin, John Morley wants the peace of mind that comes only with a sense of definition. Like Stalin, Morley goes outside himself for that definition and in the process robs himself of a real identity: "I'm losing all those faculties that identify me as a human entity! I am being transformed by some hideous force! I am hardening! I am literally hardening into some abstract reality!" (92). As bizarre as Morley was when we first saw him flouncing around the office, he was a human being, complete with free will and the ability to feel joy as well as pain. Corporate law may have given Morley a sense of transcendence, but what he has transcended is his own humanity. He is, at the end, a man without will or identity apart from the corporation.

What gives *The Latent Heterosexual* its life is its humor and its endearing picture of John Morley. Typically, Chayefsky focuses on Morley alone, and all other characters are foils. John is at first outrageous, but it is clear that his childlike defiance is part of the necessary defense of an extremely vulnerable man. He has spent his life searching for transcendence through meditation, through drugs, and through the mask of the buffoon. His desire is not so much

religious as an all-too-human wish to rise above the complexes and
fears that make him a man: "I defend myself, you see, by all these
theatrical excesses! I play mad so even my madness will seem a
deceit! But I'm terrified it may be my only incontrovertible frag-
ment of reality!" (25). While the corporation gives John a stable
identity, it does not remove the "fragments of terror which is the
human condition" (8). Once John's "theatrical excesses" are removed, once his idiosyncrasies are replaced with machine-like efficiency, he is left with nothing between him and that terror.
Chayefsky has managed to capture John's growing anguish in a
series of short, effective scenes, the most moving of which is without
any dialogue:

"Morley is alone onstage, sitting in his frozen posture at the head of the
conference table, an arm rigidly up, pen poised like a dart. For a long
moment, he simply sits this way. Then, suddenly, despite the fact the
polished table before him is desolate of any paper, Morley's arm comes
down, he scrawls with his pen, the arm goes up, a fractional pause, then
down, scrawl, up, down, scrawl, up. Then as the whole mechanical ritual
continues, tears begin to track down Morley's cheeks and, in a moment, his
shoulders shake with sobs. Grunts of anguish escape from the distraught
man. And all the while he sobs and weeps, his right arm goes up, down,
scrawl, up, down, scrawl." (79)

Despite the fantastic nature of the scene, Morley's anguish is deeply
felt.
    John makes his entrance as a comic character in a play which is
essentially filled with comic stereotypes, for they are as mechanized
in their own way as John will become. Christine may feel compassion for John, but she also insists upon feeling the private parts of
every man she encounters: her life's work is curing impotent men,
and she goes about that task with missionary zeal. The lawyers and
accountants are just that — the human element has totally left them
and has been replaced by the godlike corporation. And only it is
personal: "I don't find it hard to understand your husband's infatua-
tion for his corporation. She's a raving beauty" (67). These
stereotypes do not belie a weakness in characterization, for their
one-dimensional nature is essential to the meaning of the play.
    The language of the play is a quagmire of jargon — jargon which
sounds like diabolical incantations. Eventually, the litany of the
accountants is the only communication Morley can hear; and only

Morley's overly theatrical language at the beginning and Christine's earthy dialogue provide relief from the endless chatter of the high priests of the corporation: "Well, he's paying fifty-two percent on his separate corporations now, and a twenty-five percent tax is obviously more attractive than a fifty-two percent bite. The point is, something has to be done. Nicholson and Mayer decided last month to make a public offering, and we've got to decide whether to accept conversion on a one-to-one basis or sell our holdings at face value" (106).

In *The Latent Heterosexual*, Chayefsky tried yet another type of theater. Like the Absurdists of the 1950's, Chayefsky begins with a Realistic setting and with relatively ordinary people; but, within this framework, he moves toward a Kafka-esque fantasy. The result is a delightful and often moving play that is marred by Chayefsky's unfortunate tendency to repeat lines too often. For example, one explanation of Morley's metamorphosis would be sufficient unless additional mention presented a new perspective on the action. But Morley explains his dilemma over and over again, and we tend to feel both tired of the redundancy and angry at the condescension that causes it. Moreover, a very effective final scene is destroyed by Morley's final speech while committing hara-kiri:

Did you ever hear the story of the man who got married to get the benefit of the joint declaration, got divorced to maintain his Liechtenstein tax status, and finally killed himself on the advice of his accountant? Well, there was once this poet — not a very good one, I'm sure — but possibly the very last of his kind — ." (115)

This speech, made directly to the audience, breaks the mood of the final scene and it tends to reduce the play to an extended gag.

When *The Latent Heterosexual* was performed in America in Dallas and in Los Angeles by a company headed by Zero Mostel, the play was not a success; and we cannot help thinking that Mostel as Morley did the play no good. Mostel is a brilliant clown, but the play demanded a more subtle approach, as the more successful production in England with Roy Dotrice proved. The play has its flaws, but it also demonstrates Chayefsky's gift for presenting with charm and perception a troubled picture of modern man. More than ever before, Chayefsky strikes the balance here between comedy and seriousness, between character and theme. As Clive Barnes wrote in the New York *Times*, "The play is undoubtedly Mr.

Chayefsky's most serious work," and "Mr. Chayefsky attacks with vigor the new materialism, with its almost religious rites of financial sanctity, and he is always pointed, and pointed in the right direction. He is also funny."[26]

Chayefsky has not had a play produced in the eight years since the production of *The Latent Heterosexual*. His feeling is that his career as a playwright is over and that he has to specialize in films which he can create for a mass audience. For him, the playwright's function is dead: "I say the poor playwright no longer has what [Arthur Miller and I] came in on the rag-tag end of. We were still considered leaders of the people. T. S. Eliot said when the moral fiber of a community disappears, the poets have to stand up. When the priests and rabbis and all the great moralizers fade, it's the writer who has to establish some kind of moral contact. Well, the playwright has fallen into disrepute along with the priest."[27] Chayesfsky's five plays show a growing trend toward his regarding drama as an expression of the writer's beliefs about the fate of the human race. His early plays closed with an expression of optimism that was never so convincing as the terror and loneliness that haunted his characters at the beginning. By the time he wrote *The Passion of Josef D.* and *The Latent Heterosexual*, his plays reflected his concern with the terrors that haunt man and with the illusions he chooses to arm himself against those terrors. Chayefsky's own attitude toward his craft gives one the key to his later plays: "Being in love gives you the illusion that life is worthwhile. Writing, you know that life is not, that it is miserable and wretched, but you can face that fact."[28] For Chayefsky, like Eugene O'Neill, man has only illusions to protect him and give him substance.

Another dimension of Chayefsky's last three plays is worth noting: they have at their core a fatalistic view of man's future. Gideon defies God and tempts the extinction of his race; the chaos of the Russian Revolution is presented as an expression of the dark side of man that can be repeated indefinitely; and John Morley's fate seems like that of his race, a race of men who will give their lives for efficiency. Chayefsky said: "I write a call to disaster,"[29] and we sense in his plays a view of history as an endlessly recurring series of disasters.

Five plays is not an awesome output; but, considered as a unit, they demonstrate Chayefsky's constant experimentation with new artistic tools. No two plays are the same in form; and, while they all have some weaknesses, they also are the work of a craftsman with a superb ear for language and with the ability, through masterful dialogue, to bring his characters to life.

Chayefsky, like many playwrights, is an eclectic. He began in the Odets-Miller school of Realism which focused on the tragedies of the common man; and he moved through confrontations with God and Brechtian parable to the thing-haunted world of Ionesco and the Absurdists. Such eclecticism is redeemed in Chayefsky by his ability to transmute the techniques of his mentors so that they become unified with his own style. While the stage has not been the most congenial platform for Chayefsky's work, these plays deserve a place in our theatrical heritage.

VI   *The Critical Battle*

During his brief career as a writer for the stage, Chayefsky had his detractors among the critics. As one would expect, he greeted critical attacks with frustration and, occasionally, rage. When a critic called *Middle of the Night* a "little play" that was saved only by the acting, Chayefsky countered with a letter to the editor of the New York *Times* suggesting that Arthur Miller's *Death of a Salesman* would probably have been given the same verdict if it had first been seen on television. Chayefsky attacked the critics' condescension toward the television writer: "I could not escape the feeling, after reading some of the reviews of my play, *Middle of the Night*, that I was being looked at as a nouveau riche who had elbowed his way into an aristocrat's home and, while the gentry were by noblesse oblige dutifully courteous, they could not help raising an eyebrow at my choice of necktie."[30] He also defended the sort of Realistic play he was writing at the time: "I believe that all the beauty some poets find in dreams can be found in the involved relationship of a middle-aged man who is concerned about impotence and a highly neurotic girl of twenty-four who devours everyone she knows in her desperate search for warmth."[31] A New York *Times* attack on *The Passion of Josef D.* led to Chayefsky's lengthy letter defending the historical validity of his presentation of the key figures in the Russian Revolution and attacking critic Howard Taubman's misreading of the play: "He has invented a political play out of an utterly unpolitical play; and his suggesting my play was a piece of political hatchet-work, an anti-Communist propaganda play to be equated with the anti-American caricatures of Stalinist theater, is entirely irresponsible and a bit of dirty pool-playing."[32]

As we have seen, there is much that is noteworthy in these plays. They quite clearly mirror the playwright's developing sense of his subject matter and his willingness to experiment with different dramatic techniques.

CHAPTER 4

The Oscar Winner

I Dedicated Insanity

IT is not surprising that Chayefsky's memories of Hollywood were not pleasant ones, for he had seen his story, "The Great American Hoax," turned into a movie that bore little relationship to his concept. It became clear to him, during his Hollywood apprenticeship in the 1940's, that the screenwriter was at the bottom of the totem pole in terms of authority and prestige unless he already had a reputation in another medium as had Arthur Miller and Tennessee Williams. Still, one clear fact that emerges from the history of the American film is that few important writers have been able to tolerate the exigencies of film writing, for the writer usually surrenders his control of the script when he has finished it. Cuts and revisions can be ordered by the producer or director without the writer's approval; and, if the writer is asked to make his own revisions, he is given very little time to do so. The result of these practices is a final product that often bears little relationship to the original script, and such cavalier treatment of writers was particularly prevalent in the days of the big studios. If Chayefsky were to express himself through the film, he would have to find a way to gain absolute control over his work.

In the mid-1950's, the motion picture industry was still under the control of a handful of major studios. The threat of television was just beginning to be felt, and Hollywood's counter-attack was a plethora of large-scale productions and wide-screen processes.[1] At the same time, the "art film" was beginning to emerge as a cinematic counter-culture. The works of such European directors as Vittorio de Sica and Roberto Rosselini and the small-scale, non-star American films like *Lili* were doing extremely well in small art theaters in major cities — well enough, in some cases, to warrant larger distribution after their reputation was established in the smaller urban houses. There was a prestige attached to an art film that, in many cases, compensated for the lack of substantial financial gain. The films were made cheaply, though they were made by men who saw the film more as an artistic medium than as an industry grinding out a "product."

At the same time, a number of Hollywood personalities began to see that they could have more control over their work both artistically and financially if they formed their own companies. They might not be able to afford gambling on the type of large-scale production that the major studios were able to produce, but they could venture into the art film world and hope to create a larger audience for these small, inexpensive, but serious ventures. One of the first such companies was formed by Harold Hecht, Harold Hill, and Burt Lancaster. After viewing the much-talked-about teleplay, "Marty," Hecht-Hill-Lancaster decided to try to buy the play for film production.

The unique terms finally settled upon clearly indicated that Chayefsky had learned his lesson about Hollywood. Chayefsky would receive for his screenplay thirteen thousand dollars plus five percent of the net profit earned by the film, a far cry from the six-figure fees usually paid by Hollywood for a successful property. It was the terms of the contract, however, that were particularly interesting; for Chayefsky was to attend all rehearsals and do all necessary rewriting himself. His director on the "Philco Television Playhouse," Delbert Mann, would direct; and the entire script had to be thoroughly rehearsed before any camera work would be done (usually a film is rehearsed and shot scene by scene). Chayefsky's contract for *Marty* is indicative of his attitude toward his film scripts: they are his creations, his conceptions, and are to be produced his way. In a medium that customarily belongs either to the director or to the business office, this attitude was unusual. More extraordinary, however, is the fact that Chayefsky was able to win himself so much authority.

Marty was shot on a budget of half a million dollars, a low figure for a movie even in the 1950's. The film was, according to its writer, "paid for with buttons and bones rather than money,"[2] and demanded some artistic sacrifices: "In *Marty*, we gave up several delightful photographic touches because we simply could not afford the fifty extras or the fact that the scene would have to be shot on

Sunday, which is triple time."[3] These sacrifices and the slim chance of a profit led Chayefsky to call the making of art films "dedicated insanity."[4] Clearly, in Chayefsky's case, the insanity led to a success that was both artistic and financial. Because Chayefsky is unique in seeing the film as a writer's medium, his films are more literate than most; and his scripts are dramas for the screen rather than mere blueprints to be fleshed out by a director. Still, it is important to note that a screenplay is quite different from writing for the theater. While the screenwriter is offered a freedom of movement impossible in the theater, he is given a different set of demands and constraints. He must keep the camera moving and his settings varied to avoid monotony. He must avoid long scenes and speeches and trust to the camera the emotional responses that would be verbalized in a drama on the stage. With his apprenticeship in Hollywood and his success in television, Chayefsky was well prepared to use the possibilities of the film to his advantage.

Only two of Chayefsky's film scripts have been published. After a brief consideration of Chayefsky's adaptations of his television and stage successes, this chapter focuses upon the most celebrated of Chayefsky's films: *The Goddess*, *The Americanization of Emily*, and *The Hospital*.

II *From Small Screen to Large*

When the Academy Awards for 1954 were distributed, the motion picture industry found itself in the unique position of granting four awards including Best Actor, Best Screenplay, and Best Picture for an adaptation of a television show. The film was *Marty*, and the result of its success was a demand for more adaptations of Chayefsky's plays. *The Bachelor Party* followed in 1957 (Gore Vidal's adaptation of "A Catered Affair" had been produced the year before); then in 1959, after success on stage as well as on television, *Middle of the Night* was released. The teleplays were adapted to the larger screen with variable results; *The Bachelor Party* seemed padded, but *Marty* and *Middle of the Night* became powerful scripts because Chayefsky took advantage of the freedom of movement that the film offered to give his stories a sense of reality that made them most affecting.

Marty, in its film realization, took on a new and powerful direction because the setting is presented as an important force in the lives of the characters. In the first shot of 187th Street on a hot summer day, the camera shows us the strange combination of the Old and the New World as the Italian women shop at the street stands and in the small stores. Throughout the film, the sense of verisimilitude that is reinforced by the location shots becomes a powerful counterpart to Chayefsky's brilliant Realistic dialogue and to his realization of character. Indeed, this sense of place transforms *Marty* from a good television script to a brilliant film.

The other additions and changes to the original script also enhance the atmosphere of the piece. The story has been enlarged by filling in details of character and action. The viewer learns more about Marty's cousin, Thomas, and his feelings of guilt at having to ask his mother to leave his house. Thomas cannot help resenting the fact that his wife Virginia cannot get along with his mother and that he has been forced to shirk a traditional responsibility. Moreover, Thomas finds his young wife inferior to his mother in many ways:

THOMAS: Who buys Italian meat any more? You think my wife buys Italian
            meat? She goes to the A & P, picks up some lamb chops wrapped in cellophane, opens up a canna peas, and that's dinner, boy.
VIRGINIA: Sure, all you wanna eat is that greasy stuff your mother makes.[5]

This closer look at Thomas and Virginia leads the viewer to apprehensions about Marty. As his mother is warned by her sister of the sense of abandonment that can result from a son's marriage, we see the conflict between the traditional mother and the modern wife that Marty may face, the conflict that is realized in the discussion between Clara and Mrs. Pilletti about Aunt Catherine:

CLARA: I don't think a mother should depend so much upon her children
                for her rewards in life.
MRS. PILLETTI: Well, maybe, that's what they teach you in New York
                University. In real life, it don't work out that way. You
                wait till you are a mother. (96)

As Thomas and Virginia present an unattractive picture of marriage, the other men's immature attitude toward women — they are to be cared for by their mothers, and they see women their age as mere objects — show why a healthy marital or nonmarital relationship is a rarity on 187th Street. Marty's friends, Ralph and Leo, are constantly talking about picking up nurses for a night of fun; but, if a girl isn't good looking and sexually available, they aren't interested. By this ethos, Marty's Clara is a failure; and Marty's interest in her is inexplicable to others who advise him to "Get ridda her. This is money inna bank" (87). The most negative comments about Clara are voiced, of course, by Marty's friend Angie whose jealousy is founded upon his dependency on Marty:

ANGIE (*angry*): Brush her. Listen, you wanna come with me tonight, or you
wanna go with this dog?
MARTY: Wadda you getting so sore about?
ANGIE: I looked all over for you last night, you know that? (131)

This confrontation and Angie's wanderings the night of Marty's meeting with Clara present a vivid picture of the latent homosexuality that dooms Angie to an unhappy, lonely life.

Certainly the most important aspect of the screen adaptation is the fuller picture of the central character. From a quiet, lonely man we see Marty blossom into a joyous, garrulous soul who surprises himself with his sudden stream of words: "Well, I'm talking again. I must be driving you crazy. Mosta the time I'm with a girl, I can't find a word to say. Well, I'm gonna shut up now, because I'm not like this usually. Usually, I . . . well, here I go again" (71). Having experienced this exhilarating liberation, Marty can never surrender to the provincialism of his mother ("She don't look like Italian to me. Plenny a nice Italian girls around" [126]); to the sense of entrapment of his cousin ("You gotta good job, you got no wife, you got no responsibilities" [120]); or to the empty wanderings of his friends with their constant refrain: "Wadda you feel like doing tonight?" Certainly, the adolescent behavior of his friends pales beside the joy of being with a woman: "I got something good here! What am I hanging around with you guys for?" (135).

Marty was not the first picture to treat urban life in a vivid, realistic fashion. We only have to think of Kazan's brilliant film *On the Waterfront* which was released two years before *Marty* and which was a triumphant piece of cinematic Naturalism; but *Marty*, unlike its unrelievedly grim predecessor, managed to celebrate the possibility of beauty in even the homeliest circumstances. The Bronx shown in *Marty* is a neighborhood of lonely, unhappy people;

but the love we see develop during the weekend that the film shows us negates any sense of inevitable entrapment. As Robert Bingham observed in *The Reporter*, "Paddy Chayefsky . . . has brought out of drab people in a drab setting the ever astounding human beauty that can never be fabricated out of glamorous girls beside swimming pools."[6] The unique formula that made *Marty* such an important cinematic event was an effective blend of a romance with a happy ending that was presented within the framework of naturalistically conceived setting and characters. After *Marty* opened at the *Sutton*, a small East Side art theater in New York, it finished a run that lasted the better part of a year; and Paddy Chayefsky had proved that simplicity and quality do not always spell disaster for a film.

The *Bachelor Party*, Chayefsky's next adaptation of his own work for the screen is not so successful; for, while the central conflict is presented more vividly than in the original, Chayefsky has succumbed to the error of padding in order to stretch a fifty-three-minute television script into a full-length film. Since Charlie and Helen now live in an ugly, low-income housing development on the East Side of Manhattan, the change in locale from a Jersey City walk-up allows Chayefsky to reinforce Charlie's sense of entrapment through shots of the prison-like appearance of a high-rise apartment complex:

EDDIE: It looks like a state hospital.
CHARLIE: It looks like a prison.[7]

Charlie's plight is also reinforced by a new character, Walter, a forty-eight-year-old who is still living the monotonous routine that Charlie so dreads. Walter has an acute case of asthma and has been told by doctors to move to the Southwest, but such a move is impossible for him:

I can't quit. Don't you understand? You don't understand. I can't quit! I got a fourteen year old girl, I don't know what time she comes in at night any more. She's so wild, these kids. I got a nineteen year old boy in college; he's going to be a doctor if I have to die. He's not going to quit school. You hear me! I worked hard to put that kid in school! I don't care if I die! I don't care! What am I going to do in Arizona? Who wants me? Who's going to give me a job? What kind of job am I going to get? I'm forty eight years old. They don't want no forty eight year old bookkeeper. They got machines from IBM. (91)

Walter spends the evening trying frantically to enjoy this night on the town, to forget his misery through liquor and compulsive laughter; but nothing can ease his anguish. As the men speed underneath the city from one attempt at fun to another, Walter breaks down and shows his life to be the realization of Charlie's worst fears: "Forty-eight years old and so what? What does it mean? What happened? What have I got? What did I make? Who needs me? So this is it. A man's life, nothing. Worry about being sick, worry about making money, worry about your wife, worry about your kids, and you're on the way to the grave from the day you're born. The days drag on, and the years fly by, and so what?" (92).

As Charlie's sense of entrapment grows, so do Helen's fears for their marriage. Through his expansion of the scenes involving Helen, Chayefsky depicts the anguish felt by the wives of these unhappy men. While Charlie and his friends have their bachelor party, his sister, Julie, tells Helen of the failure of her marriage to a man who is frustrated by responsibilities of maturity: "He's a boy, my Mike. Till the day he dies, he'll never be more than fifteen. Perpetual adolescence, that's the curse of the professional man. He spends his whole youth trying to be a doctor, a lawyer, an accountant. Then he spends the rest of his life looking for the fun he should have had when he was a boy" (62–63).

Mike's sense of entrapment, which manifests itself in a string of petty infidelities that are painful and humiliating to his wife, began with an unwanted child that dashed his hopes of becoming a surgeon; for, as his wife explains, ". . . then I'm pregnant. He had to quit, what do you think? He wanted to be a surgeon, he wound up being a G.P. From that day he hated me. I had two other children by him, but he hated me. He told me in just so many words. Why do you think I kept telling you, Helen, why do you think I kept telling you: 'Don't have a baby till Charlie finds himself' " (57). Julie's experience leads her to suggest that Helen have an abortion in order to save her marriage: "My children are the only things in my life now, but I'd rather have a husband" (63).

While this idea is distasteful to Helen, she timidly offers Charlie the possibility of her not having a baby; and Charlie's serious consideration of this prospect is frightening to his loving wife who reminds him that "You're my husband, Charlie. This is your baby too. That doesn't mean anything to you. For the first time in our marriage I feel I can't depend on you, Charlie — I'm not important to you" (100). But nothing seems important to a man whose life has lost all significance. By this time, Charlie has even decided to quit night school, his one chance for upward mobility, for education now seems but another fetter. Drunk, frightened, and depressed, Charlie has lost all hope: "I don't care what I do either" (101).

This deepening of the relationship between Charlie and Helen and the addition of Walter strengthen the film, but much of what is presented as the men wander around New York is inessential. Chayefsky has added a Greenwich Village party replete with picturesque Bohemians, an unlikely place for these men to appear, and an unnamed female denizen of the Village who is known only as "The Existentialist." In her frantic search for companionship and activity, she is a female counterpart of Charlie's bachelor companion, Eddie; but she is also a foil for Helen, Charlie's wife. Charlie tries to start a liaison with "the Existentialist" who wants the right words attached to her meaningless sexual activity: "Just say you love me. You don't have to mean it" (111). While this attitude provides a nice dramatic contrast to Helen's real devotion, Chayefsky has given it to a cardboard creation that seems out of place in the story of these men. More piquant is the prostitute the men find for Arnold, the prospective groom; for her self-respect leads her to assert her respectability: "Listen, I don't want you to think I don't have a job. I got a job. I work" (83). This brief professional encounter is to be Arnold's first sexual experience, but, overcome with shame and fear, he runs out of the room.

Like the teleplay, the film of *The Bachelor Party* is most successful in its portrayal of the anguish of these young bookkeepers, the sense of the unrelieved monotony of their lives. As usual, Chayefsky has portrayed these men with dialogue that is strikingly realistic. The film has its affecting parts, but it does not engage an audience as *Marty* did. Perhaps Arthur Knight best assessed the film's virtues and failings in his *Saturday Review* comment:

To Paddy Chayefsky's credit, his instinctive feeling for character has not hardened into formula. His concern is for the individual members of the class that he knows best, not with the caricature of easily recognizable types. As a result, his plays . . . depend for their effect upon the intrinsic interest of their people. Marty, Chayefsky's "ugly butcher," for example, achieved a spread and intensity of identification that probably astonished even his creator. On the other hand, the five young men of *The Bachelor*

Party. . . . would seem to lack much of Marty's appeal simply because they are so very typical. Indeed, perhaps the basic weakness of this ambitious and complex film is the fact that there are five main characters, producing at once a diffuseness of structure and an inconsistency of focus. . . . Its heroes are simply nice little guys — whereas Marty was a *person*. [8]

The artistic problems were exacerbated by a lack of audience interest in a film which cost almost twice as much to produce as *Marty. The Bachelor Party* marked the end of Chayefsky's association with Hecht-Hill-Lancaster but hardly that of his career in films.

The screenplay for *Middle of the Night* was the love story's third incarnation, for its success on television with E. G. Marshall had led to a Broadway hit with Edward G. Robinson and finally to a film with Frederick March and Kim Novak as Jerry Kingsley and Betty Preiss. As with *Marty*, the changes made in transferring the play to the screen were all for the better. For example, the addition of scenes at Jerry's business, the Lock-Lee Company, a garment manufacturing firm, does much to define Jerry's world and to put the relationship of Jerry and Betty in a clearer perspective. The film opens at the offices of Lock-Lee, and we first see Betty in her professional role as one of the secretaries in the outer office. Her world is one of dull routine in a drab Seventh Avenue loft, but we see from the outset that something is seriously troubling her as "a sudden, heavy look of weariness, almost pain, flashes on her face."[9]

Jerry Kingsley is one of the partners in Lock-Lee, and he is first seen with his business associates discussing the deaths of mutual friends. While the discussion seems a favorite pastime with the other middle-aged men, it is clearly disturbing to Jerry: "Well, these are the years. Everybody starts dropping dead around you. I don't know. I'm standing in the shop here, cutting a pattern, when suddenly I'll think: 'My God, I'm fifty six years old. I'll be an old man with white hair pretty soon. My life is coming to an end.' It seems like everybody's in the hospital, everybody's sick, everybody's retiring" (3). He is upset, too, that his only pastime seems to be visiting his grown children, an activity that offers him little independence or gratification. In contrast to Jerry's life is that of his partner, Walter Lockman, whose character is developed considerably from the play in which he is first discussed but is never seen. Lockman fights his age by asserting his masculinity with any available "tootsie." While Jerry's friends think that Lockman's behavior

is undignified, Jerry regards Lockman's life-style to be merely
another way to cope with age: "To me visiting your children every
night seems just as disgusting" (7).

After meeting Betty, listening to her problems with her husband,
and recognizing her expression of her unfulfillment, Jerry takes his
usual trip to see his daughter; but he is fighting his temptation to
entertain the attractive young Betty. He does not want to become
another Lockman, but the temptation is too strong, and eventually
Jerry asks Betty to join him after work for dinner. The central portion of the film, the romance of Jerry and Betty and their problems
with their families, is much the same as in the play. However, Betty
succumbs to her husband's attempts to win her back sexually; and
she has a painful confrontation with Jerry in Central Park. Betty tells
Jerry that since she has slept with her estranged husband, she thinks
it better that they end their relationship, and Jerry agrees:

No, you're not a slut. You're a baby. Every time life gets a little tough for
you, you want somebody to take you in their arms, anybody, some guy in
the street, and rock you to sleep. And now you've been a naughty little girl,
and you want me to scold you and then give you a big hug. I can't take it,
kid. I'm an old man and I can't take it any more. All I want is some peace. I
don't want problems any more. You would break my heart every day of my
life I've got left. I don't want to see you any more. I'm getting out of here
before there's nothing left of me at all. (108)

Betty's weakness with her husband and her upset at losing Jerry
make the nature of her need for him clear: she needs a father figure,
a protector. She is a child, but exactly this aspect of her personality
makes her relationship with Jerry possible.

As Jerry tells his sister that he is giving Betty up, he receives a call
that Lockman has taken an overdose of sleeping pills in a hotel
room. Jerry goes to the room to be with his partner's family and talks
with Lockman's son:

LOCKMAN'S SON: Look what he's doing to my mother. He runs around with
                those cheap floozies. A dirty old man. He could be taking
                it easy now, at his age. He could be living in peace.
JERRY: Who the hell wants peace? You can have all the peace you want
        when you're dead. Your father wanted life. He wanted love, even if
        he had to pay money for it. What the hell is wrong with everybody?
        All they want is peace, comfort and security. No problems. Life is

> problems. Heartache. Passion. A woman. Love, sonny boy, no mat-
> ter how dirty and sordid and sick it may seem is still a beautiful
> thing. Everything else is nothing. (115)

Betty's love may be childlike, but Jerry's is that of a lonely, aging
man who wants the life that only love can bring. The "sweet torture"
of his affair with Betty is worth more than the emptiness of his life
without her. He returns to her, aware of her immaturity, but aware
that their vulnerability intensifies their feeling for one another.

Chayefsky has been wise to add nothing to *Middle of the Night*
that does not deepen our understanding of Jerry and Betty.
Lockman is a device to bring out Jerry's loneliness, just as Betty's
night in bed with her estranged husband and its aftermath have
emphasized her vulnerability and her need for the understanding
and stability that Jerry can provide. The focus has been kept on the
lovers, on their need for one another, and on the clash between
Betty's fear of hurting Jerry and his fear of being hurt. The freedom
of the film camera allowed the addition of situations and locales that
placed Jerry and Betty in a larger context, and what we see of their
daily lives makes their need for love all the stronger. *Middle of the
Night* was, however, the last of Chayefsky's television plays to be
adapted to the screen. By the time it was released in 1959, he had
not had a play produced on television for four years. By 1959, he had
also proved himself capable of creating powerful, original
screenplays with his award-winning production, *The Goddess*.

III   The Goddess

Chayefsky's concern in his early films was to keep the writer in
artistic control of his script, a concern that motivated the stipula-
tions he placed in his contracts with other producers and which
motivated him in 1957 to form Carnegie Productions, an independent production firm that would allow him absolute control over his
material. The result, given Chayefsky's ego and his protective attitude toward his conception, has led, unfortunately, to the use of
weak directors like John Cromwell and Arthur Hiller, who would
not fight the writer but who also could not create films with much
visual interest. Chayefsky's dual role as producer and writer led to a
great many tempestuous scenes as the writer fought with everyone

to preserve his concept of the film. One former colleague was once
quoted as saying that "Paddy is an expert on everything. You'll find
he has expertise in directing, selling, photography, promotion,
sales — everything it takes other people fifteen or twenty years to
learn. A real octopus that man — has to have a hand in everything."[10] Given the present film situation in which every actor
thinks he can direct, it seems that Chayefsky's only presumption
was in assuming that a writer could have the same prerogative as a
Dennis Hopper or a Jack Nicholson.

The first Carnegie Production was *The Goddess*, "an awfully good
film"[11] according to its creator. Its director was John Cromwell, a
Hollywood veteran who had spent many years with David O.
Selznick and who had such films as *Anna and the King of Siam* to his
credit. Unfortunately, he was not able to give any rhythm or visual
poetry to Chayefsky's script. But, despite its weak direction and its
awkward editing, *The Goddess* is often studied in college film
courses as a prime example of the Naturalistic character study that
American film makers have created so successfully. Though the film
lacks the visual impact of Orson Welles' masterpiece, *Citizen Kane*,
it is similar in its probing of the personal tragedy underlying what
seems on the surface to be a success story; but, where Kane was a
millionaire tycoon, based loosely on William Randolph Hearst, the
central character in *The Goddess* is a movie star whose life bears
many similarities to that of Marilyn Monroe. Both characters are
spiritual cripples, however.

The Goddess has its roots firmly in American Naturalism in its
uncompromisingly objective study of the inevitable deterioration of
an emotionally maimed human being. We are given every person
and incident we need to understand Emily Ann Faulkner, but
Chayefsky never lets the focus waver from his central character. To
emphasize the inevitability of Emily Ann's tragedy and to underscore its causes, Chayefsky has arranged his scenes in a cyclical
structure. When we first see her, she is a poor, unwanted four-
year-old girl; it is the Depression; and her mother's husband (not
Emily's father) has recently committed suicide after failing in the
dry cleaning business in Tennessee. Emily's mother is a nervous
young woman traveling to her brother's house in Maryland to try to
give away her daughter. Like many of Tennessee Williams' women,
Lorraine Faulkner cannot stand the thought of a drab life: "I'm only
twenty six years old! I still got my figure. I want to have a little

fun."[12] "A little fun" means a life without responsibility — no job and no child: "I don't want her! I don't want her! I was seventeen hours in labor with her, and she's been trouble ever since! I didn't want her when she was born, and I don't want her now!" (13).

Despite her desire for freedom from responsibility, Emily's mother has to stay in Beacon City and support her unwanted child; and what we see of Emily's childhood is lonely and unfulfilling. She and her mother live in squalor in the worst section of town. Emily's poverty keeps her from having white friends; her position as a Southern white in a black neighborhood isolates her at home; her mother, deprived of her chance for a life of freedom, has become a cold woman who tolerates the drabness of her life by finding solace in a fundamentalist religion that prefers judgment to love. Because Emily is ignored, she, like many lonely children, turns more and more to her imagination for emotional satisfaction. Emily's dream world is that great American fantasy factory, Hollywood, the products of which allowed millions to escape the sadness of the Depression. Emily's life is filled with movie magazine stories about the stars, and she can lose herself totally in a Ginger Rogers film.

More and more, these dreams compensate for her loneliness. As a teenager, she can get dates only by letting boys do things with her that they couldn't do with the "nicer" girls. The one occasion in Emily's life that brought her real joy was the night she appeared in the Dramatic Club play:

Everybody just came over to me and was so nice. Miss Gillespie said I was the best girl she ever had in the Dramatic Club. Well, I was so scared. I was just saying words. I didn't know I was doing anything special. Everybody was so nice to me. I began to cry. Just all of a sudden I began to cry. Miss Gillespie, she said, "What are you crying about?" I said, "I don't know. Everybody's so nice to me." . . . Well, I'm going to tell you, we went home, my mother and I — I just didn't want to go home at all that night. I was up in the clouds. But we finally went home, and my mother gave me a hug. And I began to cry all over again. . . . I do believe that was the first hug she gave me in I don't remember — since I was an infant, I believe. (28)[13]

This night intensifies Emily Ann's dreams of Hollywood which are now dreams of her own success: "I'm going to Hollywood some day and I'm going to be a star. I'm going to be a star" (38).

Her pilgrimage to Hollywood is preceded, however, by an unhappy wartime marriage to the son of a Hollywood star; and John

Tower, Jr., is as lonely and as starved for affection as Emily Ann. A soldier at a nearby base, John finds in Emily the first human warmth he has ever felt in his lonely, alcoholic life. When Emily first meets John, he is drunk after an unsuccessful suicide attempt because of his despair that blinds him to any meaning in life: "And what was it all about except worry and tears? . . . Why bother? It all ends up in the grave. You might as well make an honest effort to get there" (48). Emily is genuinely moved by Tower's loneliness, a pain akin to her own; but she is also drawn to him because he is the son of a movie star. Emily wants marriage with this troubled man despite his warnings: "You have a passion for respectability and I have a horror of loneliness — that's love! . . . The worst thing that could happen to us is if we get married. I'd hate you before the blush of the ceremony had gone from your cheeks" (55). Tower's bitterness and alcoholism make a happy marriage impossible, and the marriage is short-lived. Emily is left like her mother fourteen years before; she is restless and saddled with an unwanted child: "I don't want it! I don't want it! I didn't want it when it was born and I don't want her now! . . . I want to be happy!" (66).

John Tower's despair should have led Emily to see that Hollywood is not, after all, a magic kingdom, but the failure of her marriage returns her to her childhood dreams of stardom. When we next see Emily, she is starlet Rita Shawn, peroxided and poured into a too-small dress. Emily's ambition drives her to "play the game" with no sense of its potential damage: she is squired by a retired boxing star, and she has her press agent let the press know that they are together. Of course, Emily regards this life as the best she has ever had: "I never had it so good as right now. I got a lot of friends, and I go to a lot of parties, and I got nice clothes. My mother writes me I'm the hero of my home town" (78). Emily is finally being noticed, and for her such attention is pure joy.

Slowly, however, she becomes aware of the price she is paying; for she finds herself in a producer's bed for the sake of a bit part in one of his films. The sense of shame she feels drives her into marriage with the boxer, a marriage that cannot succeed.[14] Emily cannot live for a man's love, for love is an emotion she has never experienced: "I don't know what love is, Dutch. I find you very physically attractive, and I guess you find me very physically attractive, but that ain't going to last very long, Dutch" (100). Emily vacillates between offers to settle down with Dutch and insistence on continuing her career. Finally Dutch, who wants a stable life and who is shattered by Emily Ann's inability to be more than a sexual partner, leaves her to her career, a career that skyrockets after a night in bed with the vice-president of a studio.

Rita Shawn, née Emily Ann Faulkner, becomes a star; but the love of the public does not fill the vacuum for a lonely, emotionally barren woman. By the time Rita Shawn is twenty-six, she is a nervous wreck; she can't stand her loneliness; but she is incapable of the sort of relationship that can fulfill her: "I can't bear to be alone. I can't bear it. I've taken men home with me who I don't rightly know for more than an hour because I can't bear to be alone at night. I wake up in the middle of the night in a sweat and my heart pounding, and I've gone down and awakened my servants and made them sit with me till morning. Life just seems unbearable to me. . . . I feel I'm going insane" (136). When Rita brings her mother to help her, the cold woman offers her desperate daughter not love but religion. For a while, this solace helps, not because Rita has had a religious experience, but because it is a bond between her and another human being: "I prayed to God to save my soul. I held my mother's hand. I remember her fingers tight on mine, and that's what saved me, her holding my hand that way" (140). When Rita's mother returns to her home, Rita interprets this action as an ultimate betrayal — as a betrayal that destroys her short-lived faith, a faith that was really directed not at God, but at her mother: "There ain't no God" (148).

In the final sequence of the film, Rita returns to Beacon City, Maryland, for her mother's funeral. Now a totally broken woman, kept together by drink and pills and by a lesbian secretary who is all the mother she ever had, Rita faces her first husband and the daughter she had abandoned thirteen years before. Her comments to her husband, John Tower, echo his to her at their first meeting: "For the life of me, I can't think of any reason to get up tomorrow morning. I can't think of anything I want or look forward to. It's all a fraud, isn't it, John?" (162). John Tower hoped that a meeting with their daughter might give Rita something to live for, some hope for the future; but Rita Shawn is too ill for such a solution: "We got her to a psychiatrist for four months. Then he said to me we were wasting our money. She's a dead woman, emotionally dead" (165). The play presents no resolution such as suicide for Rita Shawn, for she will continue eking out her survival until there is less than nothing left.

But her daughter, through the love and dedication of John, will have the chance that John and Emily Ann both missed.

Chayefsky manages throughout his screenplay to avoid cliché or melodrama. The audience never merely sympathizes with or pities the heroine; it is always conscious of the larger design and its ramifications. The nightmare vision the author has created is that of a world devoid of love, a world symbolized by Hollywood, a fantasy city in which impersonal sex has replaced human feeling. A woman's marketability is based on her ability to arouse sexual fantasies: "She's got what I call the quality of availability. She's not particularly pretty. It's a kind of warmth that some women have that makes all the men in the audience think they could make her if they only knew her" (117). This empty society creates the fantasies for an entire nation, fantasies that were the only excitement in the life of a poor, lonely, unloved girl from Beacon City, Maryland. Stardom would bring her all the love and attention she lacked; little Emily Ann would finally be noticed. There would be no more parties to which she would not be invited, no more need to let the boys take advantage of her just so that she could have a date. However, what we see in Emily Ann's life is that things never change for her. From being "loose" in order to get a date, Emily moves to being "available" so she can get a part in a film and seem "available" to thousands of anonymous, lonely men. From living a lonely life, isolated and bolstered by fantasy, Emily "grows up" to a world filled with isolated, lonely, miserable people. When the old fantasies fail, she uses pills and liquor to kill her pain.

If Chayefsky's story only showed that the dreams of wealth and glamour which are symbolized by Hollywood are empty, the film would be merely a re-telling of an old story. However, Chayefsky's film begins with that assumption, and it looks for the source of the dependency upon the illusion. The source can be seen in the people who surround Emily: her mother, who wants fun and freedom and who is incapable of love for husband or child, turns to a hard, loveless religion when her dreams are shattered; John Tower, Jr., reared in the fantasy factory, hates life because it is so lonely and is incapable of love because he never was given it; Emily's friend Joanna, the victim of her mother's ambition, is an alcoholic at twenty; and Dutch, who wants a stable life but is consumed with loneliness. No one is capable of reaching out to another person, yet all are dying from a lack of love. Deprived of love, all are eaten alive by self-hate. The saddest aspect of these characters is that when they are offered love, they cannot understand or appreciate it; for, as Rita says to Dutch: "What do you mean you love me, Dutch? . . . Why should anybody love me? I don't think very much of myself. If I was a man, I couldn't love me. . . . I think I'm ugly. I'm dirty. I don't understand why you love me. I think you're physically attracted to me. I don't even know that. Why'd you marry me, Dutch? I came over any time you called me anyhow" (99). Rita is finally left with the love of a mother surrogate, a middle-aged woman who loves her shattered charge, a person to whom Emily Ann is "baby": "But I kind of love her and I'll take good care of her" (166). As the film ends on the day of Emily Ann's mother's funeral, it becomes clear that Emily Ann's mother had never lived and, as a result, we see another dead woman, her daughter.

The Goddess marks a greater sense on Chayefsky's part, of what the camera can tell without dialogue. In his earlier films, dialogue did everything but establish time and place and give the story the requisite atmosphere; but Chayefsky uses the camera in *The Goddess* to convey the crucial moments in Emily Ann's life. Perhaps no scene tells more about Emily Ann's childhood than the one in which she looks for someone to share her pride in her report card. For minutes the camera follows her through lonely streets and into the drab, desolate apartment where her only confidante is a stray cat. Emily's loneliness in Hollywood is established in a long series of shots in which we see her wandering aimlessly around the city after an assignation with a producer, and the silence during this scene emphasizes the loneliness and emptiness that by this time seem overwhelming. The sequence ends with Emily taking her first drink while her alcoholic roommate is in a stupor: "LONG SHOT *looking down the length of the living room to the two starlets sprawled on their seats, the small disarray of a small drunken binge on the carpet in front of them. Not a word is said for a long moment*" (89).[15] Chayefsky is also conscious of the telling contrasts of light and darkness, for the crucial moments in Emily's life are presented in an almost blinding light, making scenes purposely resemble "*an overexposed snapshot*" (65); and the final scene is to be "*swallowed up in the darkness*" (167).

There are a number of built-in problems to a film like *The Goddess*. Since the film is dominated by a sense of inevitability, there is no suspense; and the lack of any real communication between people also denies the possibility of a dramatic conflict. Moreover, Emily Ann's story is told through a series of unrelated vignettes which range over twenty-seven years; but this basic rejection of the usual film story line is compensated for by the intensity of each scene and by the careful arrangement of scenes. The film has a three-part structure. Part I, "Portrait of a Girl," ends with Emily echoing her mother's rejection of her in the first scene and her desire, like her mother's, for a carefree life: "I want to be happy!" (66). In Part II, "Portrait of a Young Woman," Emily's empty assignation with a producer drives her to marry Dutch; but, at the end of the marriage, we find her making another assignation with a film executive. Part III, "Portrait of a Goddess" has only two sequences. In the first, Emily Ann renounces her mother: "Nothing I do pleases you. Nothing I ever did pleases you. All you know is to run off on me. I hate you so much I can't find words to tell you how much. You never cared whether I lived or died" (146). In the final scene, Emily's mother has died, she has been replaced by Emily's loving companion, and Emily rejects her own daughter. We see Emily at the end in the room in her aunt's house in Beacon City, the room she occupied as a little girl while her mother tried to leave her with her uncle. Emily is asleep in the last scene in the same bed that she slept in in the first scene; she has gotten nowhere, gained nothing: "I'm the same as I was then and I'll always be the same, the same miserable little girl wandering through ugly streets in her high ankle shoes" (159).

The Goddess never had the success it deserved. Kim Stanley's performance offers us a record of a great, terribly underrated actress; the supporting cast is superb; and the screenplay is one of the finest original scripts of its decade. The film is still shown on television and on college campuses, despite the fact that it never earned the celebrity of *Marty* or *Middle of the Night*; and it is one of the few Chayefsky screenplays to be published in book form. Chayefsky's introduction says little about the film but much about the economics of art films in general; and these economic considerations probably led Chayefsky to wait fourteen years before producing another original screenplay.

IV   The Americanization of Emily

It may be unfair to call *The Americanization of Emily* an adaptation, for it turns a weak, pointless novel into a witty argument against man's glorification of war. William Bradford Huie's novel, *The Americanization of Emily*, published in 1959, recounts the romance between Emily Barham and James Monroe Madison, a novelist who serves as "dog robber" to an admiral during the months preceding the Normandy invasion. Huie's Madison is a pallid imitation of the Hemingway hero, an individualist and something of a fatalist: "To me life is essentially private. A man demands of himself; he doesn't seek purpose in a party or a sect or any organization. He refines his personality, which is all he has. He consoles his fellows. He chuckles when he can, gets drunk when he must. He strives, yearns, dreams — and interrupts his life to help put out fires."[16] During the month before D-Day, Madison meets Emily Barham, a driver who has tried to avoid being Americanized — showered with good food and clothes in return for sleeping with American officers. Emily and Barham pursue a matter-of-fact romance punctuated with some conflict between Emily's optimism and Madison's cynicism; and Emily indicates their difference: "You want to view and analyze; I want to believe and belong."[17] Despite the loss of father, brother, and husband to the war, Emily cannot succumb to pessimism. Before D-Day, Madison is assigned to make a movie showing how the navy played an important part in the invasion. He makes the film successfully and returns home to Hawaii where Emily joins him after the war.

If this synopsis sounds colorless, it is because Huie's novel is colorless. Madison, who narrates the book, is lifeless except for an occasional streak of pomposity; and the novel is totally devoid of conflict or suspense, the usual saving features of hack work. No doubt Hollywood was interested in the book because Huie's *The Revolt of Mamie Stover*, also about James Monroe Madison, had been made into a profitable film and because there was renewed interest in films about the Normandy invasion after Darryl F. Zanuck's *The Longest Day*. Huie was asked to adapt the novel for the screen; but his screenplay was as pallid as his book. Martin Ransohoff, the film's producer, hired Chayefsky to rewrite the screenplay; and the result is the work of an alchemist.

James Monroe Madison, the introspective intellectual "dog robber" who plays Chopin for the admirals, is changed to Charlie Madison, a raffish, brash "ugly American" who enjoys his role as "con-man" and as procurer for the admiral's staff. Before the war, Madison was not a novelist; he was the assistant night manager of a

diplomatic hotel in Washington. Since the job had involved providing more than a room for the visiting celebrities, Madison had received good training for his present military position. When World
War II came, Madison was offered a job on Admiral Jessup's staff;
but he chose active duty instead: ". . . I had always been a little
embarrassed by my job at the hotel and wanted to do something
redeeming. Have you noticed that war is the only chance a man gets
to do something redeeming? That's why war's so attractive."[18]
Madison's desire for redemption leads him into the fray at Guadal-
canal where he realizes how war could transform timid, cowardly
men into gallant heroes: "Hell, war isn't hell at all. It's man at his
best, the highest morality he is capable of" (45). Madison also
realizes, while ducking Japanese bullets in the swampy islands of
the South Pacific, that he is a coward, and that cowardice is the
antidote to war: "You see, cowards don't fight wars. They run like
rabbits at the first shot" (46). Madison returns to America; loses his
wife, who wanted a hero; and joins the Admiral's staff where he
could spend the war safely arranging behind-the-lines parties and
assignations.

A month before D-Day, Madison meets Emily Barham, an English driver who has lost every man in her family, including her
husband, to the war, and who resents the Americans' attitude:
". . . it's all one big Shriners' Convention for you Americans, isn't
it?" (12). Unlike the other young women in the motor pool, Emily has
been avoiding the American staff parties with their ensuing assignations and lavish rewards. Emily has realized that she is too much a
sentimentalist. She requested transfer from the hospital corps because her sympathy for the wounded soldiers led to too many fruit-
less nights in bed. The war has cost her too much, and she guards
her emotions, carefully avoiding any sort of involvement with men
with whom she might become emotionally involved. She wants no
more tragedies: "I've lost a husband, a father and a brother in this
war. When my husband was killed, I almost went insane. I take
these things badly. I fall in love too easily, and I shatter too easily. I
don't want any more doomed men" (19). Fortunately, Charlie Madison seems anything but doomed; and Emily finds herself attracted
enough to this cowardly but roguish character to walk into his
bedroom after one of his parties: "I've had it with heroes, Charlie"
(31). While Emily hopes at the outset that their relationship will be

only an affair, it is clear that these two cynics are made for one another.

Madison's life at this point couldn't be happier. He has a position that keeps him happily out of the fray, and he has met his match. This situation, however, is only the beginning of Chayefsky's screenplay; for the dark comedy he invents out of the bare bones of Huie's novel is a witty, outlandish satire on the war mentality that Madison so despises. For Madison, wars are pursued because they offer man a chance to be heroic: "It's not war that's insane, you see; it's the morality of it. It's not greed or ambition that makes wars; it's goodness. Wars are always fought for the best of reasons, for libera-tion or manifest destiny, always against tyranny and always in the interests of humanity. . . . As long as valor remains a virtue, we shall have soldiers" (47). To Madison, the generals do not create wars, but "the rest of us who make heroes of our dead and shrines of our battlefields" (48).

Like anything built upon destruction, war is also insane, as Madi-son learns all too well. His Admiral, in the throes of a nervous breakdown, decides that a film must be made showing that the first man killed on Omaha Beach was a sailor; and this bizarre footage is to be incorporated into a plea to the senate for more naval appropri-ations. While the staff sees the film as the product of a sick mind, the Admiral has written the President about it, and the web of bureau-cracy makes the film a necessity. Charlie is put in charge of the filming, a position he tries to refuse because ". . . this movie is just an unnecessary piece of naval public relations, and I won't risk my life for that" (82). But the prospect of such a noble endeavor as storming the beach at Normandy with a movie camera has Madi-son's Annapolis-trained superior, Bus Cummings, so excited that there is no way to escape the assignment. Moreover, Cummings wants the movie made so he can avoid telling his children that he was in a London hotel room during the Great Invasion (poor eyesight has kept him unhappily committed to a desk job).

Charlie's machinations to avoid going to Normandy turn even Emily against him: "Since you are cowardly, selfish and ruthless, I can't help but despise, detest and loathe you" (92). Madison gets on the ship, joins the thousands of men charging the beach, but turns and runs the other way at the sound of German gunfire. His superior, Cummings, shoots him in the leg, which sends Charlie

hobbling toward the beach where he trips on a land mine and is
presumed to be the very thing he went to film — the first sailor
dead on Omaha Beach. The news of Madison's death does not make
Emily feel ennobled: "We no longer take pride in death in this
house, Bus. What was admirable about Charlie was his sensation of
life — cowardly, selfish, greedy appreciation of life, unadorned and
uncertain as it is" (123). That very appreciation of life makes Charlie
almost invincible, and he surprises and horrifies the naval public
relations men — who have plastered his picture and the story of the
noble death of the first sailor killed on Omaha Beach in every newspaper and magazine in America — by returning to Southhampton
alive.

Madison's anger at the hoax of his heroism makes him want to tell
the whole bizarre story to the press — from about the mad Admiral
to the gunshot wound his fellow soldier gave him when he ran the
other way. He will risk prison to expose the fraud of war, but Emily,
now "Americanized" by Charlie, sees his craven survival as superior
to noble sacrifice: "War isn't a fraud, Charlie; it's very real. At least,
that's what you've always tried to tell me, isn't it? — that we shall
never get rid of war if we keep pretending it's unreal. It's the virtue
of war that's the fraud, not war itself. It's the valor and self-sacrifice
and goodness of war that need the exposing. And here you are,
being brave, self-sacrificing and absolutely clanking with moral fervor, perpetuating the very things you detest, merely to do the right
thing" (142). At the end, Charlie is falsely painted a hero, but he has
Emily whom he has Americanized into believing, as he does, that:
"Life isn't good or bad or true; it's merely factual; it's sensual; it's
alive" (94).

The Americanization of Emily was written during the period in
which Chayefsky was spending most of his time writing plays, and
the screenplay has much in common with his stage work. Like
Gideon and *The Passion of Josef D.* (also written in 1963), *The
Americanization of Emily* is a "problem play" that uses characters
and scenes to argue a thesis. In fact, Charlie Madison, though seemingly the typical American rogue, bears much resemblance to the
garrulous hero of one of Shaw's plays — the man who turns his
personal philosophy into a religion which he not only lives but
preaches at every possible opportunity. Charlie, like his Shavian
forbears, is an iconoclast preaching the downfall of hollow, destruc-

tive platitudes in favor of a pragmatic view of life: "So I preach cowardice. Through cowardice, we shall all be saved" (47). Yet, like Shaw's heroes, he ultimately is bested at his own game by a clever woman who understands him — and life — better than he does. The livelier scenes in the film are not scenes of action but of arguments which are vitalized by Chayefsky's sparkling dialogue. While such scenes might seem static in a film, Chayefsky is clever enough to vary the pace and tone of his screenplay.

In contrast to the witty dialogue of the Falstaff-like debates on honor, the film also gives us a deft satire on the perverse ideals that Charlie so despises. Admiral Jessup, mad as a hatter, is far more worried about the army's gaining more prestige than the navy than he is about defeating the Germans. The Annapolis graduates on his staff fight with the less prestigious men on active duty. Bus Cummings is ashamed of having a desk job rather than an opportunity to perform a valorous act on the battlefield and goes so far as to challenge Madison to a duel when the latter refuses to make the film. Madison is shot not while taking Normandy but while filming an incident that will help the navy in its rivalry with the army. Certainly the bizarre happenings on the admiral's staff demonstrate Madison's thesis about the sickness of war. In the face of the actions and motivations of those around him, Madison's cowardice does seem to be a shining virtue.

Characteristically, Chayefsky considers the honor of war to be merely another illusion that gives man's life some meaning. Charlie's claim that there is no truth, only fact, sounds much like Lenin's comment in *The Passion of Josef D.*: "Nothing is real. Nothing is true. The human condition is relentlessly uncertain."[19] The only honest approach to life is to live according to pragmatic facts, not immutable truths; for, to Chayefsky, such truths get man into trouble. Valor cannot be a beautiful emotion if it kills people, and life is the most important fact of all.

The screenplay is an interesting prelude to the sort of black comedy that Chayefsky was to write in *The Latent Heterosexual*, in that the background is peopled with amusing caricatures that underscore the world view of the central character. The mad admiral, the overzealous aides, the dotty old woman who refuses to believe that her husband and son are dead — these grotesques create not only an interesting background but also living proof of the philosophy of the

central character. Many of these secondary characters remind us of
the zany personages of Joseph Heller's *Catch-22*, a novel that presents much the same view of war as *The Americanization of Emily*.

Typical, too, of Chayefsky's writing during this period is the alternation of the brilliant flights of rhetoric of the central characters
with the parodies of the clichés of the world they inhabit. Just as *The
Latent Heterosexual* parodies corporate jargon and *The Passion of
Josef D.* mocks revolutionary cant, this film uncovers the absurdity
of the sort of language that we usually accept in war movies as being
heroic:

MADISON: Bus, I — don't know how to say this, but — I'd like another
chance. I'd like to apologize for my contemptible behavior before, and — well, I've packed my gear, and — well, we've got a
job to do, and I'm ready to do it.

CUMMINGS: (*with a proud smile*) Underneath it all, you're a pretty gutsy
guy, Charlie, aren't you?

MADISON: I don't know what came over me before. I showed the white
feather, I suppose.

CUMMINGS: (*gripping Madison's shoulders*) Forget about it, Charlie. (88)

If the dialogue alone is not absurd enough, Chayefsky undercuts this
exchange by placing it in a hotel room in which Cummings' over-
night female visitor is sitting undressed on the bed and filing her
nails.

A character in the original screenplay for *The Goddess* tells Emily
Ann that the only books he reads are "a few slim volumes of Mark
Twain's black little pessimism,"[20] and we cannot help being reminded while viewing *The Americanization of Emily* of Twain's
hatred of what he called "the moral sense," that faculty of arrogant
self-righteousness that leads men to "inflict pain for the pleasure of
inflicting it,"[21] the faculty responsible for most human cruelty.
Charlie Madison echoes Twain when he responds to Emily's threat
to leave him because of his cowardice by saying: "You've done the
morally right thing. God save us all from people who do the morally
right thing. It's always the rest of us who get broken in half" (96).

John Russell Taylor, in his book, *Cinema Eye, Cinema Ear* wrote:
"Even today in the films scripted by Paddy Chayefsky there is no
doubt that Chayefsky's rather than his various directors' is the dom-
inant personality."[22] We see Chayefsky's effectiveness more clearly
in this film than in any other; for beginning with a weak novel,

Chayefsky conceived a point of view and then totally remolded the characters and the situations to exemplify it. The result is that rarity — a witty, literate script which, as Bosley Crowther wrote, . . . "says more for basic pacifism than a fistful of intellectual tracts."[23]

V The Hospital

In a career as successful as that of Paddy Chayefsky, a career that is still in process, it is somewhat dangerous to speak of a work as the culmination of it, but *The Hospital* is just that — the finest statement of the ideas that have so far pervaded all of his work. A daring film in its mixture of varied tales and tones, *The Hospital* is a vision of the nightmare that modern man has created for himself.

Chayefsky's hospital, set in the midst of Manhattan, exists on two levels. It is, first of all, a beleaguered city hospital, understaffed and overcrowded; plagued from within by insensitive staff and bureaucratic inefficiency and harassed from without by every segment of the community, all of whom want the hospital to be run their way and to be independent, of course, of any practical consideration of human or financial cost. The pickets and protests about hospital expansion reach the boiling point, yet we see an institution that cannot meet the needs of the community without that expansion. The hospital is not helped, either, by doctors who are more interested in making a million than in their patients; by residents more interested in "zapping" nurses than in proper diagnosis; or by the self-proclaimed "bitch from the accounting office" who will let patients die rather than receive treatment before giving her their Blue Cross number. The depiction is frightening because it is quite familiar, but Chayefsky's film is not only a satire on one of our more problematical, though well-meaning, institutions.

On the second level, Chayefsky's hospital is a frightening image of contemporary life in a violent, loveless world; for it is the institution in which we see most clearly the illness of our culture. In one frightening scene, the audience sees the emergency room not merely as a department of a hospital but as the end result of a sick world when old Mr. Drummond catalogues what is collected in that chaotic mass of pained people: "The kid swiped by a car, the old fag beaten by sailors, the asthmatic lady who collapsed in the subway, the teen-aged suicide, the paranoids, the cut-up dudes, the drunks, the rapes, the septic abortions, the overdosed addicts . . . the fractures, infarcts, hemorrhages, concussions, boils, abrasions, the colonic cancers, the cardiac arrests — the whole wounded madhouse of our times."[24]

But not only in the emergency room do we sense the chaos of contemporary society; for, when the protestors finally corner the director of the hospital, he shouts back: "You run it! You pay the bills! You fight the city! You fight the state! You fight the unions! You fight the community! You think you can do it any better? — you do it! I'm just going to tell you one thing! This is a sick society and a dying world, but we don't have any cures for that here! And you don't have any cures for it either, baby!" (130).

The chaos of the hospital is also enhanced by occasional but horrible lapses into incompetence. The film begins with the story of a man who comes into the hospital with chest pains and, in the course of less than twelve hours, is mis-diagnosed and drugged to death. He dies, not of his chest pains, but of CO_2 narcosis. This victim of ineptitude shared Room 806 with another victim of a system that does not have time to be careful. This victim, Dr. Drummond, a former Harvard physician who became a religious fanatic and lives with the Apache Indians in Mexico, came to the hospital for a physical examination. He walked in in good condition; but, within a week, he was nearly dead as a result of some gross errors in judgment on the part of the staff.

Drummond, however, is not so sick as the staff presumes — at least, not physically. In a vision, he saw his late roommate who claims to be God and who orders Drummond to avenge his death by killing the doctors and nurses who had mistreated him. Drummond works the revenge in the most effective way by creating situations in which the guilty staff members become patients and are then killed by professional ineptitude. Dr. Shafer, an oversexed resident, is killed when mistaken for a patient; and Dr. Ives is given a shot that produces a heart attack, is taken to the emergency room, and is left to die without treatment. Nurse Campanella, after having been hit over the head by Drummond, and placed unconscious in a patient's bed, is prepped for an operation; given a shot that, when combined with anesthetic, would kill her; is exchanged for a patient outside an operating room; and dies on the operating table because no one had checked to make certain that the right patient had been sent in.

In a world of bureaucratic institutions, there is no time to check on the human being behind the number: "In a point of fact, she died because she was wearing another woman's identity. Like the others, she was overlooked to death. Surely, that is God's revelation — that in a man-made world, man himself is the only thing that is truly without value" (112). The result of a society comprised of such institutions, institutions which, in the name of efficiency, reduce people to numbers, is "the great American plague — vestigial identity" (111). Fittingly, old Drummond escapes from the hospital when the staff thinks that a doctor who is having a coronary attack in his room is he. The hospital does not even recognize its own staff.

Living in the chaos that Chayefsky sees as our world cannot help but be hellish for a sensitive person. The central character of *The Hospital* is the most effective realization of Chayefsky's typical hero — the man who is struggling to regain the sense of meaning without which "the only admissible matter left is death" (61). Dr. Herbert Bock has just separated from his wife after twenty-four unhappy years of what he calls a "sadomasochistic dependency" (23). His children have gone the way of the urban affluent: the son has become a Maoist "building bombs in basements as an expression of his universal brotherhood" (23), and the daughter has had two abortions and has been arrested for selling drugs at a "rock" festival. Bock is angry and guilty about his failings as a husband and as a father: "I blame myself for those two useless young people. I never exercised paternal authority. I'm no good at that" (24). His worst problem, however, is that he is tortured by a sense of impotence — not of sexual impotence, the fear of which he sees as a national obsession, but of the impotence created by the loss of a sense of meaning: "When I say I'm impotent, I mean I've lost even my desire for work, which is a hell of a lot more primal a passion than sex. I've lost my raison d'être, my purpose, the only thing I've ever loved" (60). With nothing left to live for, Bock attempts suicide.

He is prevented from injecting himself with a lethal dose of potassium by the beautiful young daughter of Dr. Drummond, the madman responsible for the strange deaths of the hospital staff. Barbara Drummond, too, is among the walking wounded; for having experienced the "obligatory" stages of growing up in the 1960's — radicalism, acid, and an affair with a member of a minority group — Barbara has a nervous breakdown. Her refuge has been the peace of the Mexican hills where she watches over her fanatical father; for, unable to cope with chaos, Barbara has completely forsaken civilization. When Barbara interrupts Bock's suicidal injection he, in a rage, rapes her on the couch in his office. The result is that Bock, after a night of real passion, realizes that he is not so dead as he had thought and that he is in love with this strange young woman. Bock wants Barbara to keep her father in the hospital and stay longer with him; but Barbara, angry at the hospital's mistreatment of her father and frightened by the deadly chaos she sees around her, asks Bock to follow her to peace in the Mexican mountains:

You're a very tired and very damaged man. You've had a hideous marriage and I assume a few tacky affairs along the way. You're understandably reluctant to get involved again. And, on top of that, here I am with the preposterous idea you throw up everything and go off with me to some barren mountains of Mexico. It sounds utterly mad, I know. On the other hand, you obviously find this world as desolate as I do. You did try to kill yourself last night. So that's it Herb. Either me and the mountains or the bottle of potassium. (73–74)

Barbara offers Bock the most attractive lures possible — love and escape — but Chayefsky is shrewd enough to see that stronger objectives exist for a man like Herbert Bock: "Somebody has to be responsible, Barbara. Everybody's hitting the road, running to the hills, running away. Somebody's got to be responsible" (132). Realizing that a man's meaning comes from maintaining his integrity, Bock stays at the hospital; to him, "running to the hills" would be as much a "cop out" as suicide.

The Hospital is, above all, an audacious work. Where Chayefsky failed in his play *The Passion of Josef D.* to combine a personal history with the larger social forces surrounding it, he has, in *The Hospital*, been able to combine a number of stories successfully. Moreover, the nightmare vision of society is presented in comic terms. The world we see is absurd, but the point of view is not the despair of the Absurdists. If Bock's story shows anything, it is the fruitlessness of despair. If any work of Chayefsky's has demonstrated his interest in "characters caught in the decline of their society,"[25] this one does. The world seems to have reached a state of incurable madness, and the options for man seem to have dwindled to two: either he departs, or he remains to fight a futile battle.

Chayefsky's early work offered the promise of meaning through love, but love in *The Hospital* is merely the combination of a sexy young woman who is attracted to older men and a middle-aged man who is looking for some means of proving to himself that he is still alive. While in *Middle of the Night* Chayefsky made a beautiful romance with such a couple, love for Bock and Barbara is nothing more than a night of passion on an office couch. Though that night does cure Bock of his despair, it does not provide him with the sense of meaning that he needs since he is enough a product of the previous generation to believe in the importance of responsible action. Chayefsky does not erase the doubt that such a belief may be an illusion because of the hopeless chaos of society, but we admire Bock's desire to continue trying to heal not only physical ills but the hospital, the manifestation of society's ills. He may be engaged in futile activity, but he is alive and constructive: "I send out eighty doctors into the world, sometimes inspirited, at least competent. I've built up one of the best damn departments of medicine in the world. We've got a hell of a heart unit here and a hell of a kidney group. A lot of people come into this hospital in pain, Miss Drummond, and go out better for the experience. So don't tell me how unnecessary I am" (72). Though Bock has failed as a husband and father — probably failed because he believed too much in the myth that affluence brings a happy family and because his work was his first love — he has accomplished something that justifies his existence and gives him a sense of meaning.

In *The Hospital*, Chayefsky combines a clear-headed vision of contemporary chaos with a plea for retaining some of the old middle-class verities that have been vilified by late twentieth-century Americans. He rejects radicalism and hedonism as self-serving, and he celebrates discipline and responsibility as being at least constructive. The radicals threaten and scream, but the middle-aged men of the Establishment run the hospital as best they can. With this support of the virtues of the middle class, Chayefsky evinces intolerance for its less praiseworthy propensity for greed and ruthlessness. If there is a villain in *The Hospital*, it is Wellbeck, the surgeon who is more concerned with money than with his patients. Wellbeck is not a doctor; he is a conglomerate. He sees medicine as a stepping stone to millions and feels himself justified not by his competence but by his money.

Above all, though, *The Hospital* exposes one of our society's favorite myths: the belief that bureaucracies are efficient. The hospital is the perfect example of the inhumanity that results when people within an institution are regarded merely as cogs in a big machine. In this film, as in *The Latent Heterosexual*, Chayefsky voices his fear of the predatory nature of bureaucracies — their ability to rob a man of his humanity: "I think one of your patients in here is dead, Dr. Spezio. Why do you say that, Mrs. Cushing? Because he wouldn't give me his Blue Cross number, Dr. Spezio" (34). Indeed, Herbert Bock suffers despair at the beginning of the film because he is too human not to be hurt by the wreckage around him. The time is out of joint, and Bock finds it increasingly difficult to fight an overwhelming sense of futility:

You know, Bruebaker, last night I sat in a hotel room, reviewing the shambles of my life and contemplating suicide. Then I said: "No, Bock, don't do it. You're a doctor, a healer. . . . Your life is meaningful." Then I came in this morning and find out one of my doctors was killed by a couple of nurses who mistook him for a patient. . . . And now you come to me with this gothic horror story in which the entire machinery of modern medicine has apparently conspired to destroy one lousy patient. How am I to sustain my feeling of meaningfulness in the face of this? (40)

Bock cares; and, unlike most of the people we see in the film, he cares about someone other than himself. He is saved by his unselfishness; and that quality in man is the saving emotion, the antidote, not for all of society's ills, but for the despair that is both their cause and their effect.

As usual, the mood and tone of the film are sustained by the brilliance of Chayefsky's language. The jargon of the hospital reminds us of that of the accountants and lawyers in *The Latent Heterosexual*. The rhythmic syllables of digitalis and pulmonary edema seem to have mystic powers of their own, and to be the modern counterpart of the Indian's thunder dance in old Drummond's room. The Latinate diseases and cures seem for most of the characters to replace real human communication. Chayefsky uses such jargon to emphasize his sense that people's loss of individualized language reflects their loss of individuality: "It was great in the old days, because in the old days there were people. They've become deodorized, sterilized, with utterly replaceable parts."[26]

The jargon of the hospital finds its counterpoint in the radical jargon of the protesters who are screaming without listening and who are reducing grave social problems to slogans and name-calling. The hospital becomes a sort of tower of Babel; and the mad ravings of Drummond, the religious fanatic, seem at least to show more perception than those of most of the other characters. Bock's dialogue, with its earthiness and its straightforwardness, is a direct contrast to what we hear from the people who surround him: "My God, the incompetence here is absolutely radiant! I mean, two separate nurses walk into a room, stick needles into a man . . . tourniquet the poor sonofabitch, anchor the poor sonofabitch's arm with adhesive tape, and it's the wrong poor sonofabitch. Where do you train your nurses, Mrs. Christie — Dachau?" (19).

Chayefsky is also daring in his defiance of some of the rules of film making. Some of the speeches are pages long, but they are so beautifully wrought that they hold the viewer's attention without much movement of the camera. While Chayefsky's control of his own screenplay avoided any artistic compromise, his use of a weak director was a bad gamble since Arthur Hiller's direction of the film makes the film unsuccessful visually. The chaos of the camera work and the sloppy cutting cannot be considered as a reflection of the chaos Chayefsky is showing us; it is merely bad direction. Despite this, *The Hospital* is a marvelous film because it displays a brilliance of wit and a soundness of judgment unusual in American screenplays. And the mastery with which Chayefsky juggles the many different stories of the characters makes the film a *tour de force*.

VI   Network

As this book goes to press, Chayefsky's latest screenplay is going into production in New York City. *Network*, like *The Hospital*, is a black comedy about the dehumanization that seems endemic to America in the late twentieth century. Unlike *The Hospital*, there is no hope offered at the end, no suggestion that there are individuals strong enough or courageous enough to fight the chaos that characterizes modern society. In many ways, *Network* has much more in common with *The Latent Heterosexual* than any of Chayefsky's other work.

The setting of *Network* is the inside of one of the most powerful forces in our society, the headquarters of a television network. Chayefsky's assumption is that television has an awesome amount of control over the information people receive and, therefore, the decisions they make. The network we see in Chayefsky's screenplay is in the throes of a corporate nervous breakdown. What emerges clearly from the totally irresponsible decisions made by the employees of the network is that any form of morality or standard of taste is irrelevant. The only arbiter of values is the almighty rating. Numbers rule everything.

Howard Beale, Chayefsky's hero, is the anchorman on the lowest rated network news program. As the film begins, he has been told that he has only another week on the air after which he will be replaced by someone who will, it is hoped, boost the show's rating. Beale's response to his firing is to inform his audience that he is going to kill himself on the air on the last show: "So tune in next Tuesday. That'll give the public relations people a week to promote the show, and we ought to get a hell of a rating with that, a fifty share easy — ."[27] The next night, Beale is allowed a moment to say farewell to his television audience (his firing was made immediate after the suicide threat), and he uses the time to inform the audience in vivid scatological terms that life is meaningless and worthless. Before he can finish his message, the red button is pushed and he is taken off the air.

Beale's suicide threat and vivid sermon the following night make his news show the top rated one and he, of course, is allowed to keep his job. His new image is to be that of "an angry prophet denouncing the hypocrisies of our times" (52), but his prophecies begin to be based on real visions and voices Howard sees and hears and he becomes more and more of a modern Jeremiah. His audience grows in size and fervor, and the network is encouraged to carry out some of their other bizarre plans, such as building a weekly show around the guerilla tactics of a real radical fringe group — weekly real bank robberies, bombings and kidnappings. This show, too, is an immense success.

Unfortunately, Howard Beale undergoes yet another conversion. After a number of messages to his audience denouncing the corporate strategies of the parent company of his network, Beale is summoned to a meeting with the Chairman of the Board. The chairman's message to Beale is a grim description of a society in the clutches of its large corporations whose only standards are monetary:

You get up on your little twenty-one inch screen, Mr. Beale, and howl about America and democracy. There is no America. There is no democracy. There is only IBM and ITT and AT and T and Dupont, Dow, Union Carbide and Exxon. What do you think the Russians talk about in their councils of state — Karl Marx? They pull out their linear programming charts, statistical decision theories and minimax solutions like the good little system analysts they are and compute the price cost probabilities of their transactions and investments just like we do. The Moslem masses may be medieval, but every moment of their lives is determined — not by some savage desert god called Allah — but by the primordial pull of profit and the primeval push of power. We no longer live in a world of nations and ideologies, Mr. Beale. The world is a college of corporations, inexorably determined by the immutable by-laws of business. (127)

The chairman's message to Beale becomes his new gospel, one that demands not anger and resistance, but sad resignation:

It's the individual that's finished. It's the single, solitary human being who's finished. It's every single one of you out there who's finished. Because this is no longer a nation of independent individuals. This is a nation of two hundred odd million transistorized, deodorized, whiter-than-white, steel-belted bodies, totally unnecessary as human beings and as replaceable as piston rods. (129)

However true Beale's new message may be, it is not as appealing to his audience as his old rage. Ratings begin to slide and producers get nervous, but Beale cannot be fired since the chairman of the board wants his gospel propagated. There is no impasse, however, that cannot be resolved by a wily television producer. Howard will be assassinated on his first show of the season by the guerilla organization that is under contract to the network. This bizarre plan disposes of Beale and boosts the ratings of the guerilla group.

The plot of *Network* is indeed bizarre, but the horrifying fact is that it does not seem unbelievable. Chayefsky sees the network as a corporate beast feeding on a confused society's anger and predilection for violence. The producer who could conceive of the televised murder of Howard Beale is not a monster; she is a beautiful woman whose emotions have been conditioned, not by people, but by television. As her lover says: "I'm not sure she's capable of any real feelings. She's the television generation. She learned life from Bugs Bunny. The only reality she knows is what comes over her teevee set" (104). The issue is not one of heroes and villains, but of individualists and people committed to the corporate ideal. There is no hope here offered for men who cannot find their identity within the world of accountants and television ratings.

Network is the most recent of a handful of screenplays Chayefsky has produced in the past two decades. Like its predecessors, it is a cogent argument for the belief that the film is as suitable a medium for the serious playwright as it is for the creative director. In a medium that is considered primarily visual, Chayefsky has dared to write literate scripts that hold the audience's attention through verbal rather than visual fireworks. As a result, Chayefsky's screenplays provide better reading than most and offer a better record of the films of which they are a part than do most scripts. A discussion of Chayefsky the screenwriter is, therefore, a discussion of a career in the process of change and growth, and we only hope that the strength of Chayefsky's output remains undiminished.

CHAPTER 5

The Activist as Playwright

C HAYEFSKY'S writing is part of an extremely active life, for he spends much of his day in an office near Carnegie Hall writing and visiting with friends in show business. His work and his interest in what is going on in the world have led to a number of interesting projects. In 1959, through the auspices of the Union of Soviet Writers and the United States State Department, he spent almost a month in Russia conferring with Russian writers. With him on the journey were such notables as critic Alfred Kazin and historian Arthur Schlesinger, Jr., who remembers that Chayefsky ". . . had a way of making mordant and amusing remarks and of clearing through the claptrap with quick, effective, answers."[1] Edward Weeks, editor of *Atlantic*, remembers the anger more than the wit: "His response to other writers was real and so swift — and sometimes so outraged. He would get almost uncontrollably angry in discussions of writing and censorship."[2] Chayefsky's outrage at the idea of censorship is a natural outgrowth of his strong sense of the integrity of an artist's work. His strong will led him into an interesting diplomatic conflict with his Russian hosts. The story is best told by Arthur Schlesinger, Jr.:

Paddy Chayefsky's parents come from a village in the Ukraine, and he hoped that he might visit their home. He communicated this hope to the Soviet Embassy in Washington and again to the Writers' Union in Moscow. In due course, a trip was laid on to Kiev, where the rest of the group would meet local writers and see the town while Mr. Chayefsky would go by automobile to his village. Then, the day before we were due to go, the trip was cancelled. The reason provided by the Writers' Union? "No hotel rooms are available in Kiev."

The reason did not seem convincing. Mr. Chayefsky pointed out that a Soviet writer, eager to visit a place near Montgomery, Alabama, would be a bit suspicious if he were told that the trip was out because there were no hotel rooms in Montgomery. He then walked over to InTourist where he was informed that there were plenty of rooms available in Kiev. Being a man of determination, Mr. Chayefsky booked passage for New York and announced that he would leave the next day unless the Kiev trip was reinstated by five o'clock that afternoon. A few moments before the deadline, hotel rooms were found and the trip was restored.

So we went to Kiev. For Mr. Chayefsky to make his pilgrimage and rejoin the rest of the party on what we were told was the last plane that evening to Moscow, it was necessary for him to leave the hotel at eight in the morning. He then could drive five hours to the village, stay an hour, and drive back to Kiev in time for the evening plane. But no car appeared at eight — or nine, or at ten, or at eleven. In a city of nearly a million, the Ukranian Writers' Union seemed unable to find a car and driver. Around noon a car at last arrived. It was pointed out to Mr. Chayefsky that, if he went now, he could not catch up with the rest of the party that evening. But Mr. Chayefsky's curiosity and determination were at a high point, and he insisted on going. Just before his departure, a new and later Kiev-Moscow plane was discovered; if he hurried, he was now told, he could still get back to Moscow that night.

He left, drove five hours, and reached the village. The villagers had never seen an American before. They greeted him with enthusiasm; people who remembered his parents appeared; preparations had already been made for a banquet. Then, after seven minutes, Mr. Chayefsky's escort reminded him that, if he wanted to make the late plane, he would have to depart. They drove furiously back to Kiev, rushed to the airport — and found that there was no late Moscow passenger plane.[3]

Clearly, an uneasy compromise had been achieved — against Chayefsky's will.

In 1971, Chayefsky was among the American delegation to the International Conference on Soviet Jewry at which he voiced his displeasure at the group's inability to agree on a policy toward the persecuted Jews in Russia. His concern for his people and for their plight in Israel led to his participation in the founding of Writers and Artists for Peace in the Middle East.

This combination of artistic creation and social activism is not unusual for a man who has always seen the writer as a social critic and as a social leader. Indeed, Chayefsky gave up writing for Broadway ten years ago because ". . . drama clearly has little social usefulness for a post-industrial society in which the function of the playwright, like that of the priest, is to provide entertainment."[4]

For Chayefsky, "The purpose of any art form is to reveal to its audience some truth about their own lives,"[5] and the playwright is akin to the prophet. "I write out of social necessity"[6] is a rather daring statement for a playwright to make, but Paddy Chayefsky is still convinced of the importance of the artist to society. While his medium and his message have changed during the years, and while he was never so doctrinaire as Clifford Odets or Arthur Miller, Chayefsky has, in his work, manifested not only his love for the individual but also his anxiety about the society that engulfs the individual. His primary theme is the de-personalization of modern American society, and his works present something of a social history of urban America.

The early works focus on the poor immigrants who inhabited so much of the tenement districts of American cities during the first half of these centuries. Whether they came to America to avoid persecution like the old man in "The Reluctant Citizen" or to fulfill their dream of a better, richer life like the Italians in "Fifth from Garibaldi," the immigrants bring with them traditional patterns that protect them from the alienating chaos of the American city. Because of such traditions, Mario Fortunato insists upon being treated with the authority of the don, the Italian head of the household; and Marty Pilletti's aunt wants to live with her married son as she would in the old country. The tension in Chayefsky's early work is, therefore, the tension between the parents' espousal of traditional forms and the children's desire for American independence. A son wants to decide on a profession independent of his father's ambitions; a daughter-in-law wants authority over her own house.

If America offers freedom from traditional structures, it also offers loneliness. The only enclaves of solidarity are the home and family, for the world outside and beyond judges people only on appearance and usefulness. Mario Fortunato finds his work in the navy yard demeaning, but he comes home to love. The old cantor in "Holiday Song" finds no sign of human warmth in the world; his faith is restored through the reunion of a husband and wife. What Chayefsky clearly mourns in his work is the loss of spiritual values and, in its wake, the loss of love and compassion; and nowhere is the gap between the Old and the New World seen so clearly as it is in *The Tenth Man*. The old men are kept alive by faith and custom; and the synagogue is truly a meeting place for them, a cultural center. Like so many of Chayefsky's old people, the men seem like orphans, forgotten people in a world in which their age makes them outcasts.

They believe in things of the spirit — God, dybbuks, love; but the modern man, Arthur Landau, believes in nothing. His only set of definitions comes from psychotherapy, but they have been of little use to a man who can no longer feel anything but pain. While the old men seem comical vestiges of another era, they feel, they believe. Nothing seems more destructive than the skepticism born of materialism.

Such skepticism dominates Chayefsky's later plays, for the author himself seems to have come to disbelieve his own happy endings. In the plays of the 1960's, Chayefsky sees only the dark side of spiritual values. Josef Stalin in *The Passion of Josef D.* seems living proof of Lenin's fear of any sort of belief. Religion, progress, humanitarianism — all only lead to murder. At the end, Chayefsky seems one with his Lenin: "Nothing is real. Nothing is true. The human condition is relentlessly uncertain. That, it seems, is the primal terror."[7] The traditional structures of the Old World are gone, as are the beliefs; and, in their place, a man settles either for the truth that there is nothing in which to believe or for an illusion.[8] There is no longer even the saving belief in the power of human love.

The Latent Heterosexual gives us a man looking for an apocalyptic experience. He finds it not in the desert but on Madison Avenue by accepting as the true faith the corporate religion of profits and tax loopholes. The result is his total dehumanization — his total loss of will and feeling. Since man has made a god of the machine, particularly the machine that computes profits, man's prime object is to become as one with his machine — efficient and unfeeling. John Morley, however, cannot lose that one basic human feeling — his terror about the essential meaninglessness of his existence. It is that terror that will separate him from the machine he seems to have become: "I would say he lives constantly exposed to the ultimate terror of life which is the existential state of all men. It must be insufferable."[9]

Chayefsky's most recent work, *The Hospital*, gives us a panoramic picture of the result of a world in which traditional structures and beliefs have been destroyed and in which man is thrown back on himself. The radicals expect institutions to perform miracles since they seem to be all that is left to believe in; however, the hospital does not even seem capable of performing its primary function of healing. Within an institution expected by society to be humanitarian and altruistic, there is no one who has the time, the ability, or the inclination to be either. Within it, too, we see the end result of a world without feeling — drug addiction, senseless violence, unwanted pregnancies. The next generation, the grandchildren of the immigrants of Chayefsky's early plays, seem filled with hate or with self-destruction.

From "Fifth from Garibaldi" to *The Hospital,* Chayefsky presents us with a three-generation picture of urban America — from idealistic immigrants to their ambitious children to their disillusioned grandchildren. From belief in the saving value of love, the author moves to an admiration for those who, like Dr. Bock, fight the battle to maintain at least the illusion of order: "Somebody has to be responsible, Barbara. Everybody's hitting the road, running to the hills, running away. Somebody's got to be responsible."[10]

We can see this progression toward disillusionment and social concern by looking closely at Chayefsky's heroes. Chayefsky's first heroes are the little men — nice, easygoing, working-class people who want some brightness in what seems to be a very grey life. Chayefsky does not paint them as victims of the corrupt socioeconomic system as does Odets, nor does he create them as the tragic victims of the illusory American dream as does Miller in *Death of a Salesman.* Chayefsky is not interested in why Marty Pilletti or Charlie *(The Bachelor Party)* are where they are; he is only interested in that which can offer them some joy. Marty and Charlie suffer from the American sickness, prolonged adolescence; but they both finally realize that there is no such thing as the freedom that married men feel they have lost. Aimless wandering is no replacement for the love of a woman.

Critics have attacked Chayefsky for ignoring the non-psychological aspects of these men's lives — can his Charley ever be happy trapped in the same dreary niche all his life? — but the author was in his early years enough of a believer in the individual spirit to feel that a man transcended his environment; a man didn't change it or succumb to it. In this sense, despite all the emphasis on Realistic depiction of environment, Chayefsky is not a Naturalist. There is always a happy ending, and that happy ending is a discovery of the transforming value of love. Anatole Shub, in a perceptive essay, comments on the celebration of love that forms the denouement of Chayefsky's early plays:

Chayefsky's message of love has some of the tone of "positive thinking" and is part of the popular culture of psychology. It soaks all real conflicts — personal or social — in a murky rhetoric of good intentions, "mutual" understanding, and self-limitation. Chayefsky's most popular works have no villains. Love's enemy is an internal state, the inability to love; and the quality of this affliction doesn't vary much, whether a man or woman are concerned, or parents and children, or whoever. In his happy endings, in which the will to love finally breaks through, much must be taken on sheer faith — wishing will make it so — and much remains open to very diverse interpretations.[11]

By the time Chayefsky created Arthur Landau, the focal figure of *The Tenth Man*, that happy ending seemed to lack some conviction. Landau's sudden ability to love seems to be the author's depiction of his need rather than a possible conversion. His rebirth seems less credible than Ellen's dybbuk.

Arthur is an early version of *The Hospital*'s Herbert Bock, the intelligent, successful man who has failed with everything that is emotional; and we see in *The Hospital* that mankind has no time for lasting emotions in the midst of chaos. Barbara Drummond is as damaged as Ellen Foreman, but a man's surrendering his life to loving her would be a selfish mistake. The heroes of *The Tenth Man* and *The Hospital*, like the focal characters of *The Passion of Josef D.* and *The Latent Heterosexual*, are no longer the simple, nonintellectual little men. Chayefsky is no longer interested in the redemption of a mundane world through love; he needs leading men who can analyze a less curable despair.

The progression from Marty Pilletti to Herbert Bock is also part of the stylistic change from "slice-of-life" Realism to the more eclectic mixture of dramatic techniques that characterizes Chayefsky's later work. Marty was a character to be watched and sympathized with; Herbert Bock must also be understood; for he, like Lenin, is the author's spokesman. Chayefsky moves, during his career, from the well-wrought Realistic vignette through the quasi-Shavian dramatic argument to a more abstract black comedy. At the same time, his focus broadens from the individual to society itself — a change that requires a less focused, more complex form of presentation.

We can see the beginning of the transition in *Gideon*, Chayefsky's first non-Realistic play. Gideon, who really is an Old Testament Marty, is a simple, homely soul who wants no great spiritual truths; he wants only food on the table and a loving family. God's miracle is realized through one of the "little men"; but, in order for Chayefsky to pursue the conflict between man and God that is the heart of the play, Gideon must become more articulate, more complex, and, in the process, become something other than the simple soul he was at the beginning of the play. The Gideon who can win an argument with God, who can say "I must aspire," has changed because of the necessities of the play, not because of an organic character transformation. Chayefsky has moved, therefore, from Realism to a more intellectualized form of dramatic debate. As a result, his leading character must become both intellectual and articulate. The same sort of character dominates *The Passion of Josef D.* since Stalin, too, begins as a little man; but he also must be a man who understands himself well enough to explain his actions to the audience and to be a proper foil for the intellectual Lenin. The result is not a character from the Realistic theater but a credible mask for the author's interpretation of a real historical figure.

Chayefsky did not have to travel a long distance from the character as persona to the character as symbol, which is what we find in John Morley, the flamboyant writer in *The Latent Heterosexual*. Morley begins as a comic character, an outrageously "campy" homosexual; but the play's meaning is developed through his metamorphoses from flamboyant homosexual to stereotyped heterosexual to asexual; from creative imagination to analytical intellect to a will-less machine. Morley is slowly de-personalized, sacrificed to the god of materialism. The principal character in *The Latent Heterosexual* is a far cry from the homely, Realistic figures of the early plays. However successfully conceived, he is an abstraction created to depict a point of view.

With Herbert Bock, Chayefsky has managed an effective synthesis of his three approaches to character. Bock, in great part due to George C. Scott's brilliant acting, emerges as a real person who is beset by all the anxieties and failures that seem to be attendant upon sensitive men. His marriage is a failure, his children disgust him, his job no longer offers him any sense of worth, and his money does him no good at all. Bock is articulate almost to a fault, but he seems to strike successfully the uneasy balance between the typical and the familiar. He is as real as Chayefsky's early characters, yet he operates within the framework of a highly contrived near-farce, and he functions as Chayefsky's own spokesman.

As a matter of fact, *The Hospital* succeeds as a fascinating synthesis of all that has gone before. Like *The Latent Heterosexual,* it presents a comic picture of de-personalization in a bureaucratic society. Through Bock's dialogues, it presents Chayefsky's favorite topic of man's sense of meaninglessness in a senseless world. Like *The Tenth Man,* it offers a romance between two people who have been injured by contemporary life, but their romance has no happy ending. The film meshes reality with fantasy, but so successful is Chayefsky at depicting his vision of a mad world that both the reality and the fantasy seem credible. We also see in *The Hospital* the other crucial progression in Chayefsky's work — that from sentimental drama spiced with humor to very unsentimental comedy.

Chayefsky's progression in genres has led to a metamorphosis in language; and his dialogue, more than any other aspect of his work, has been praised even by his detractors. In the early plays, critics were constantly commenting about Chayefsky's uncanny ear for urban speech. In reviewing *Middle of the Night* in 1956, Walter Kerr wrote that "As fans of *Marty* know, this desultory poet of middle-class life has a way with an overheard phrase. The language comes out in stammering, rhythmic repetitions ('Well, how do you feel? Feel all right?'); in blurts of primitive folksy philosophy ('You had a good marriage with George — you paid the rent and went to bed, what more do you want?'); in sketches of wonderfully irrelevant information ('I called you at three in the morning — New York time.')."[12]

Unfortunately, some critics associated Chayefsky's ability to re-create urban language with a lack of selectivity and of a really creative imagination. What these detractors did not see was the careful control that Chayefsky exerted over his language to give it the proper balance of banality and eloquence. Not surprisingly, Chayefsky became tired of being associated with tape recorders and with newspaper reporters rather than with playwrights; and he began to make his own feelings known. As he told one set of reviewers, "I'd like to find a tape recorder as clever as I am in dialogue."[13]

After *The Tenth Man,* Chayefsky's style began an interesting series of transformations that resulted in a style far better suited to the richness of his later plays, if one less vivid at delineating social types. In *Gideon,* Chayefsky tried a highly stylized quasi-poetic language for his Old Testament characters. The vocabulary is rich, often ornate (a characteristic of all of Chayefsky's work in the 1960's);

and the language rolls along rhythmically, though without very much imagery. It does not have the overly mannered quality of MacLeish's *J.B.*, but neither does it have the beautiful imagery that redeems the latter play.

From the poetry of *Gideon*, Chayefsky moved to the crackling dialogue that makes *The Americanization of Emily* such a vibrant script. The contrast between the brash Madison and the cautious Emily makes their scenes fascinating, comic confrontations; and the subtle parody of military clichés is successfully presented. As a matter of fact, the basis of much of Chayefsky's dialogue in his three recent comedies is parody of the jargon of American institutions: the military expressions of bravery and honor; the legal-financial jargon of *The Latent Heterosexual;* and the medical mumbo-jumbo of *The Hospital.* The minor characters in each work become one with their jargon. Clichés seem to come to life and to threaten those who would oppose them.

Chayefsky's style has remained fairly constant since *The Americanization of Emily* in which the vocabulary is extremely rich and constantly indicates a fascination for words. Chayefsky told one interviewer, "I collect words the way some people collect postage stamps;[14] and we sense his delight at the mere sound of a good line. We find certain favorite words — "piquant" seems to be the most common example — thrown into a dialogue merely to have the characters savor the word itself:

EMILY: That's a piquant thing to say, wouldn't you agree?
MADISON: Yes, I think I'd call that piquant.[15]

or, from *The Tenth Man:*

SCHLISSEL: That was a very piquant statement, wouldn't you say?
ARTHUR: Yes, I think I would call it piquant.[16]

The result of this fascination with the sound and variety of words is a rich, highly literate language. If we combine this language with a fine, acerbic wit and spice it with a mastery of the well-timed colloquialism, we have the dialogue that characterizes and illumines Chayefsky's work. We need only cite one of Bock's monologues in *The Hospital* to discover the richness of the language used within a series of brief, simple sentences — a breathless effect that reflects the man's rage, but a rage that cannot quench his wit: "I have a son, twenty three. I threw him out of the house last year. Pietistic little humbug. He preached universal love and despised everyone. He had a blanket contempt for the middle class, even its decencies. . . . His generation didn't live with lies, he told me. Everybody lives with lies, I said. I grabbed him by his poncho, dragged him the full length of our seven room despicably affluent middle-class apartment and flung him out. I haven't seen him since."[17]

A few months after *The Hospital* opened, Walter Kerr wrote a paean to Chayefsky's language in the film:

This is my week to hate Paddy Chayefsky. I hate Paddy Chayefsky because he has just dumped a whole tubful of hard driving, candid, scratchily sophisticated dialogue into a film when the film doesn't need it all and the stage is starved to death for it. . . . Blunt language . . . agitated language (George C. Scott screaming at length in an open doorway, racing to get his rancor out before it throttled him), meaningful language (the people kept talking until they'd found out what they did want), informed language (the people seemed to live on the planet and not to have been processed in the studio). By the time Mr. Scott, brilliant as ever and thinking matters through freshly scene by scene, got around to a blistering, self-mocking, society-baiting harangue capped by a clenched fist and a savagely imperti-nent slogan ("I'm impotent. I'm proud of it. Impotence is beautiful!"), I was in a state of despair.[18]

The present Chayefsky is much more likely to be compared to a thesaurus than to a tape recorder, but one thing is clear — he is, at present, the best writer of dialogue that the American theater has to offer.

As Chayefsky seems absolutely exuberant about language itself, so do his recent scripts suggest a man bursting with things he wants to show us and with ideas he desires to share with us. The result can be a marvelous experience like *The Hospital* or a hodgepodge like *The Passion of Josef D.*, a play with great moments that also lacks the focus it needs to allow such bright moments to shine.

Paddy Chayefsky is now at the height of his powers as a writer. He has moved from the area of sentimental, Realistic comedy to satire; and he has, in the process, become one of the few living dramatists with the combination of perception and wit that is needed if the playwright is to follow in the path of the great writers of comedies of manners. His theme is the chaos that man has made of his world through his lack of perception or through his failure to accept any social responsibility. His targets are those bastions of American faith: the military, the corporation, and the hospital — and the crime that they all perpetrate is the robbery of individualism. Where Chayefsky began his career by glorifying the good heart of the "little man," he now attacks the institutions that have robbed people of their identity and their dignity. He is not interested in what he calls the "vogueish youthful philosophy"[19] of violence but in the assertion of individual responsibility. In the face of a "collapsing society,"[20] he has moved from objective Realism to a far more personal style — to one that reflects his feeling that "Writing has become more and more interior with me now."[21]

Chayefsky now calls himself "a playwright who has no theater,"[22] for he has forsaken the legitimate stage for the greater freedom and wider audience offered by the film. The results so far have been fascinating, but the film medium seems alien to such verbal eloquence. As Walter Kerr commented: *"The Hospital* could have been made with half its words, film's verbal requirements are so minimal. So many tend to clot the screen; it's on stage they're free to flow openly, like a cut vein."[23] Yet, through the film, more audiences can appreciate one of the few satirists left in our civilization. Moreover, Chayefsky can serve the film by showing that a place exists in that too-often illiterate medium for fine writing as well as for artful direction.

Clearly, whatever medium Chayefsky chooses to work in, he is still one of our finest talents. Six years ago, Richard A. Duprey wrote that Chayefsky ". . . still appears the leading strongman of our currently productive dramatists. We may say this because in Chayefsky's work there's a genuine humanistic commitment, an effective eclecticism as regards technique, an ability to see humor as an effective and credible counterpart to the most serious of problems, an understanding of what's bothering the contemporary Jew and a physical and intellectual vigor that promises additional years of creativity."[24]

Now more than then, Duprey's praise seems justified. Chayefsky may have abandoned the stage to Neil Simon and David Merrick's highly marketable commodities, but he is now a vital force in a medium that is just beginning to realize its artistic potential. As

Chayefsky once told a group of colleagues, "We all aspire to some form of posterity. The most modest of us would like to think that in fifty years — if the continents are still here — people will look at our work and say 'Ooooh!' To become the rage in fifty years is more important than now to a writer."[25]

Notes and References

Chapter One

1. Transcript of an interview by John Clum with Paddy Chayefsky, February 28, 1973.

2. Quoted in J. P. Shanley, "Big Decision on a Bronx Gridiron," New York *Times*, December 12, 1954, Sec. II, p. 15.

3. Quoted in Helen Dudar, "Paddy Chayefsky: A *Post* Portrait," New York *Post*, January 4, 1960. I am also indebted to Chayefsky and to Eleanor McKay of the Wisconsin State Historical Society for their help in ordering this section.

4. Quoted in Dudar, "A *Post* Portrait," January 5, 1960.

5. *Ibid.*

6. *Ibid.*

7. Shanley, "Big Decision on a Bronx Gridiron."

8. Paddy Chayefsky, "Fifth from Garibaldi," Typescript in Paddy Chayefsky Papers, Wisconsin State Historical Society. All further references are to this text.

9. Clifford Odets, *Golden Boy* (New York, 1937), p. 42.

10. *Ibid.*, p. 214.

11. "A Few Kind Words from Newark," Typescript in Chayefsky's possession, p. 1. All further references are to this text.

12. "The Giant Fan," *Harper's Bazaar*, No. 2967 (February, 1959), 111. Further references are to this text.

Chapter Two

1. Quoted in "A *Post* Portrait," January 6, 1960.

2. *Television Plays*, p. xii.

3. Bernard Kalb, biographical study of Chayefsky, *Saturday Review*, XXXVIII (April 16, 1966), 13.

4. Quoted in Kalb sketch.

5. Rod Serling, Introduction to *Patterns* (New York, 1957), p. 35.

6. Tad Mosel, Introduction to *Other People's Houses: Six Television Plays* (New York, 1956), p. ix.

7. Quoted in Shanley, "Big Decision on a Bronx Gridiron."

8. *Television Plays*, p. 81. All further references to Chayefsky's published teleplays are to this text.

9. "Good Theatre in Television," *How to Write for Television*, ed. William I. Kaufman (New York, 1955), p. 46.

10. "The Reluctant Citizen," Working script in Paddy Chayefsky Papers, Wisconsin State Historical Society, p. 13.

11. "The Sixth Year," Working script in Chayefsky's possession, p. II-10B. Further references are to this text.

12. "Catch My Boy on Sunday," Working script in Paddy Chayefsky Papers, Wisconsin State Historical Society, p. I-33.

13. The film version of "A Catered Affair" was the only script Chayefsky sold outright to a producer without any conditions. Gore Vidal wrote the screenplay.

14. "A Catered Affair," Working script in Chayefsky's possession, p. I-17. All further references are to this text.

Chapter Three

1. *Middle of the Night* (New York, 1957), p. 23. All further references are to this text.

2. Henry Hewes, "The City Around Us" (review of *Middle of the Night*), *Saturday Review*, XXXIX (February 26, 1956), 26.

3. S. Ansky (Solomon Rappaport), *The Dybbuk*, trans. Henry G. Alsberg and Winifred Katzin (New York, 1926), p. 49.

4. *The Tenth Man* (New York, 1960), p. 82. All further references are to this text.

5. Robert Brustein, "Love Does It Again" (review of *The Tenth Man*), *The New Republic*, CXLI (November 23, 1959), 21.

6. Anatole Shub, "Paddy Chayefsky's Minyan: *The Tenth Man* on Broadway," *Commentary*, XXVIII (December, 1959), 526.

7. Kenneth Tynan, review of *The Tenth Man*, *The New Yorker*, XXXV (November 14, 1959), 21.

8. Anon., review of *The Tenth Man*, *Time*, LXXIV (November 16, 1959), 57.

9. Gore Vidal, "The Couch in the Shrine" (review of *The Tenth Man*), *The Reporter*, XXI (December 10, 1959), 30.

10. "The Book of Judges," *The New English Bible* (Oxford/Cambridge, England, 1970), p. 277.

11. *Ibid.*, p. 281.

12. *Gideon* (New York, 1962), p. 19. All further references are to this text.

13. Quoted in "Man and His God," *Newsweek*, LVIII (November 20, 1961), 69.

14. *Ibid.*, p. 69.

15. Robert Brustein, "All Hail, Mahomet of Middle Seriousness" (review of *Gideon*), *The New Republic*, CXLV (November 27, 1961), 21.

16. Susan M. Black, review of *Gideon*, *Theatre Arts Magazine*, XLVI (January, 1962), 10.

17. *The Passion of Josef D.* (New York, 1964), p. 107. All further references are to this text.

18. "Preliminary Notes for The Passion of Josef D," Typed transcript in Paddy Chayefsky Papers, State Historical Society of Wisconsin, p. 30.

19. *Ibid.*, p. 51.

20. *Ibid.*, p. 51.

21. *Ibid.*, p. 190.

22. *Ibid.*, p. 11.

23. Henry Hewes, "The Dispassion of Paddy C." (review of *The Passion of Josef D.*), *Saturday Review*, XLVII (February 29, 1964), 26.

24. Draft of letter from Chayefsky to Howard Taubman, drama critic of the New York *Times*, February 24, 1964, Paddy Chayefsky Papers, State Historical Society of Wisconsin, p. 12.

25. *The Latent Heterosexual* (New York, 1967), pp. 17–18. All further references are to this text.

26. Clive Barnes, review of *The Latent Heterosexual*, The New York *Times*, March 22, 1969, p. 52.

27. Horovitz, Laurents, Chayefsky, Melfi, quoted in "An Ad Lib for Four Playwrights," *The Dramatists Guild Quarterly*, V (Winter, 1969), 18.

28. *Ibid.*, p. 5.

29. *Ibid.*, p. 15.

30. "Not So Little," New York *Times*, July 15, 1956, Sec. II, p. 1.

31. *Ibid.*

32. Draft of a letter from Chayefsky to Howard Taubman, drama critic of New York *Times*, February 24, 1964. Paddy Chayefsky Papers, Wisconsin State Historical Society.

Chapter Four

1. Cinemascope, the wide-screen process that could be used with conventional equipment, was introduced in 1953 as a counter to the small home screen. Before that, there had been some use of a three-dimensional process requiring special glasses and resulting in a headache.

2. Preface, *The Goddess*, (New York, 1958), p. x.

3. *Ibid.*, p. xi.

4. "Dedicated Insanity" is the title of the Preface to *The Goddess* when it appeared as an article in *Saturday Review*, XL (December 21, 1957), 16.

5. "Marty," Working script in Chayefsky's possession, pp. 120–21. All further references are to this text.

6. Robert Bingham, "Passion in the Bronx" (review of "Marty"), *The Reporter*, XII (May 5, 1955), 36.

7. *The Bachelor Party* (New York, 1957), p. 95.

8. Arthur Knight, review of *The Bachelor Party*, *Saturday Review*, XL (April 27, 1957), 25.

9. "Middle of the Night," Working script in Paddy Chayefsky Papers, Wisconsin State Historical Society, p. 1.

10. Quoted in Dudar, "Paddy Chayefsky: A *Post* Portrait."

11. Preface, *The Goddess*, p. xiii.

12. *The Goddess*, p. 13. All further references are to the published text.

13. A problem in discussing *The Goddess* results from the fact that a considerable portion of Chayefsky's script had to be cut for economic reasons. The entire sequence comprising pp. 80–90 of the script, a sequence that provides the motivation for Emily Ann's marriage to Dutch Seymour, was cut, among others. In my discussion, I refer to the published script rather than to the film itself; for the cut sequences are crucial to the story line. I shall note when I am discussing a passage that is *not* in the film.

14. This entire sequence is not in the film.

15. This, too, is not in the film.

16. William Bradford Huie, *The Americanization of Emily* (London, 1960), p. 13.

17. *Ibid.*, p. 14.

18. "The Americanization of Emily," Working script in Chayefsky's possession. Further references are to this text.

19. *The Passion of Josef D.* (New York, 1964), p. 99.

20. *The Goddess*, p. 52.

21. Mark Twain, "The Mysterious Stranger," in *The Mysterious Stranger and Other Stories* (New York, 1962), p. 193.

22. John Russell Taylor, *Cinema Eye, Cinema Ear* (New York, 1964), p. 10.

23. Bosley Crowther, review, of *The Americanization of Emily*, The New York *Times*, October 28, 1964, p. 51.

24. "The Hospital," Working script in Chayefsky's possession, p. 109. Further references are to this text.

25. Quoted in McCandlish Phillips, "Focusing on Chayefsky: 'Make it Picture Maker,' " The New York *Times*, January 3, 1972, p. 32.

26. *Ibid.*

27. "Network," Shooting script courtesy of Paddy Chayefsky, pp. 10–11. Further references are to this text. Since this is a preliminary shooting script and will inevitably undergo a number of revisions before production and post-production editing of the film are completed, I have given only an outline of the work and have deferred making an evaluation of a work still in progress.

Chapter Five

1. Quoted in Dudar, "A *Post* Portrait," January 6, 1960.

2. *Ibid.*

3. Arthur Schlesinger, Jr., "The Many Faces of Communism," *Harper's Magazine*, CCXX (January, 1960), 54–55.

4. "Has Broadway Had It?" New York *Times*, November 23, 1969, Sec. II, p. 7.

5. *Ibid.*

6. From transcript of an interview by John Clum with Paddy Chayefsky, December 22, 1972.

7. *The Passion of Josef D.* (New York, 1964), p. 99.

8. In an interview with John Clum, Chayefsky compared his present attitude to that of Eugene O'Neill — that illusion is necessary for any sort of peaceful rapprochement with life.

9. *The Latent Heterosexual* (New York, 1967), p. 113.

10. "The Hospital," Working script, p. 132.

11. Anatole Shub, "Paddy Chayefsky's Minyan: *The Tenth Man* on Broadway," *Commentary*, XXVIII (December, 1959), 523.

12. Walter Kerr, review of *Middle of the Night*, New York *Herald Tribune*, (February 9, 1956), quoted in *New York Theatre Critics Reviews*, XVII (1956), 372.

13. Quoted in Dudar, "Paddy Chayefsky: A *Post* Portrait."

14. Quoted in McCandlish Phillips, "Focusing on Chayefsky: 'Make it Picture Maker,' " The New York *Times*, January 3, 1972, p. 32.

15. "The Americanization of Emily," Working script, p. 33.

16. *The Tenth Man* (New York, 1960), p. 43.

17. "The Hospital," Working script, p. 59.

18. Walter Kerr, "I Hate Paddy Chayefsky," The New York *Times*, April 2, 1972, Sec. II, p. 1.

19. McCandlish Phillips, "Focusing on Chayefsky: 'Make It Picture Maker,' " p. 32.

20. *Ibid.*

21. *Ibid.*

22. *Ibid.*

23. Kerr, "I Hate Paddy Chayefsky," p. 3.

24. Richard A. Duprey, "Today's Dramatists," *American Theatre* (London, 1967), p. 217.

25. Horovitz, Laurents, Chayefsky, Melfi, "An Ad Lib for Four Playwrights," p. 19.

Selected Bibliography

PRIMARY SOURCES

1. *Published Works*
(with Israel Horovitz, Arthur Laurents and Leonard Melfi). "An Ad Lib for Four Playwrights," *The Dramatists Guild Quarterly*, V (Winter, 1969), 4–19.
The Bachelor Party (screenplay). New York: New American Library, 1957.
"The Giant Fan," *Harper's Bazaar*, No. 2659 (February, 1959), 122–23, 183–86.
Gideon. New York: Random House, 1961.
The Goddess. New York: Simon and Schuster, 1958.
"Good Theatre in Television." *How to Write for Television*. ed. William I. Kaufman. New York: Hastings House, 1955. pp. 44–48.
"Has Broadway Had It?" The New York *Times*, November 23, 1969, Sec. II, p. 7.
The Latent Heterosexual. New York: Random House, 1967.
Middle of the Night. New York: Random House, 1964.
"Not So Little," The New York *Times*, July 15, 1956, Sec. II, p. 1.
The Passion of Josef D. New York: Random House, 1964.
Television Plays. New York: Simon and Schuster, 1955. Includes "The Bachelor Party," "The Big Deal," "Holiday Song," "Marty," "The Mother," "Printer's Measure," and Chayefsky's essays on his work.
The Tenth Man. New York: Random House, 1960.
2. *Unpublished Works*
   Entries followed by a (W) are housed in the Paddy Chayefsky Papers, Wisconsin State Historical Society. Others have been consulted thanks to Paddy Chayefsky and are in his possession.
"The Americanization of Emily." Final working script (1963).
"Catch My Boy on Sunday." Working script (1953). (W).
"A Catered Affair." Working script (1955).
"A Few Kind Words from Newark." Rendering for screenplay (1949).
"Fifth from Garibaldi." Typescript of play (1952). (W).
"The Hospital." Working script (1971).
"Marty." Working script for film (1954). (W). I have used Mr. Chayefsky's copy containing his final revisions.
"Middle of the Night." Working script of film (1959). (W).
"Network." Working script of film (1975).

Preliminary Notes for *The Passion of Josef D.* Typed transcript (1963–64). (W).

"The Reluctant Citizen." Working script (1952). (W).

"The Sixth Year." Working script (1953).

In addition to the above, all the notes and drafts housed in the Paddy Chayefsky Papers, Wisconsin State Historical Society, have been consulted. The collection comprises most of Chayefsky's work up to 1964.

SECONDARY SOURCES

Since no other full-length study of Chayefsky's work exists, the following listings either provide useful background or contain discussions of specific works by Chayefsky.

BRUSTEIN, ROBERT. *Seasons of Discontent*. New York: Simon and Schuster, 1965. Includes reprints of Brustein's lengthy reviews of *The Tenth Man* and *Gideon*.

DUDAR, HELEN (with Sally Hammond and Jack Fox). "Paddy Chayefsky: A *Post* Portrait," The New York *Post*, January 4–7, 1960. Fine four-part series on Chayefsky's life and work up to 1960.

DUPREY, RICHARD A. "Today's Dramatists." *American Theatre*. London: Edward Arnold, 1967. pp. 209–24.

GOLDSTEIN, MALCOLM. "Body and Soul on Broadway." *Modern Drama*, VII (February, 1965), 411–21.

KERR, WALTER. *The Theater in Spite of Itself*. New York: Simon and Schuster, 1963. Includes discussion of *The Tenth Man*.

LAUFE, ABE. *Anatomy of a Hit*. New York: Hawthorn Books, 1966. Discusses Broadway hits since 1900 — including *The Tenth Man*.

LEWIS, ALLAN. *American Plays and Playwrights of the Contemporary Theatre*. New York: Crown Publishers, 1970. In one chapter, "Man's Relation to God," Lewis discusses *The Tenth Man* and *Gideon* and compares them to MacLeish's *J.B.*

MOSEL, TAD. *Other People's Houses*. New York: Simon and Schuster, 1956. This edition of Mosel's teleplays includes interesting background essays on television drama.

New York Theatre Critics Reviews. This invaluable publication offers weekly reprints of all major New York newspaper reviews of Broadway and Off-Broadway productions. It was the source for my reading of contemporary newspaper reviews of Chayefsky's plays: *Middle of the Night*, XVII, (1955), 370–73; *The Tenth Man*, XX (1959), 232–35; *Gideon*, XXII (1961), 174–82; *The Passion of Josef D.*, XXV (1964), 354–57.

New York Times Theatre Critics Reviews, 6 vol. New York: 1970. Contains all *Times* reviews of Chayefsky's films.

SERLING, ROD. *Patterns*. New York: Simon and Schuster, 1957. Another collection of famous teleplays; containing interesting background essays about television drama.

SHUB, ANATOLE. "Paddy Chayefsky's Minyan: *The Tenth Man* on Broadway," *Commentary*, XXVIII (December, 1959), 523–27. Interesting, lengthy discussion of the play.

STURCKEN, FRANCIS WILLIAM. "An Historical Analysis of Live Network Television Drama from 1938 to 1958." Unpublished doctoral dissertation, University of Minnesota, 1960. Good survey of television dramas with an emphasis on the so-called "Golden Age of Television."

WEALES, GERALD. *American Drama Since World War II*. New York: Harcourt, Brace and World, 1962. In one chapter, "The Video Boys," Weales dismisses Chayefsky and his fellow converts from television.

Index

147